OPEN AWARENESS
OPEN MIND

finding lasting peace with the practice of meditation

Karma Yeshe Rabgye

ISBN: 978-93-83296-48-4

Breathing in
I calm my mind

Breathing out
I relax my body

May I be focused
May I be at peace

I would like to thank everyone, past and present, who

played a part in this book. I truly appreciate your

teachings, advice, guidance and encouragement.

Other books by this author:

The Best Way to Catch a Snake

Life's Meandering Path

Ripples in the Stream

Reflections – Wisdom for the 21st Century

All available on Amazon and Kindle

Contents

Foreword

Karma Yeshe Rabgye is a Buddhist monk. But don't let that put you off. He hasn't been recognised as any great reincarnation. We have no need to place him on a throne and bow down to him. To be honest if you did he would feel very uncomfortable. He's not the 6th of this or the 14th of that. He is not a lineage holder of some secret mystical tradition going back hundreds of years. In many ways he is just like you or me.

He had a normal upbringing and through his own efforts built up a successful career in the City of London with all the perks and benefits that came with it. He could do or buy pretty much whatever he wanted to. Surrounded by all the symbols of success that our society aspires to, he had made it. The great western dream.

We can't walk down the street, look at a television screen or glance at our mobile phones without being bombarded by images promoting this dream. External success, wealth, status and the so-called happiness that go with it. These images move us to be hyper-productive, to consume more than we really need or can even afford. We proudly show off our newly acquired purchases to anybody around us who cares to pay attention. To an impartial observer it might seem as if happiness depends on having more stuff.

Yeshe, like many of us, came to realise that this dream didn't live up to the hype. It simply isn't enough. You could call it a blessing, but the sudden onset of illness left him bedridden. Forced to spend hours looking at a hospital ceiling led to the realisation that things had to change in his life. Whatever he had achieved brought him no lasting happiness. Only a hollow sense of momentary satisfaction. He saw clearly that he was caught in a rat race that only brought temporary highs and lows. No peace of mind at all.

In a radical move that left many of his family and friends scratching their heads in disbelief, Yeshe left behind his prosperous life in London and found himself at the feet of many great Buddhist teachers and meditation masters in India and Nepal. Like many others he benefited from the mass exile of Tibetan masters following the oppression of their religion in Chinese occupied Tibet. Fearing that their sacred traditions would be lost they were keen to pass on their treasures of wisdom.

After receiving hundreds of hours of teachings, Yeshe was extremely fortunate to be invited to live in a monastery in the Himalayan foothills of India. This allowed him to continue to study and meditate on the teachings he had received while repaying the monastery's kindness by running their office. Living in the monastery he quickly understood the daily reality of most of the monks around him. Many spent their time performing ritual ceremonies and had little knowledge of the Buddhist philosophy he had been so generously given. Most monks never even meditated.

Out of this understanding Yeshe's career as a teacher began. Encouraged by the head Lama, Yeshe began to teach meditation and basic Buddhist philosophy to the monks. By all accounts these classes were a great success. His open, questioning approach to the teachings brought them alive and inspired many monks to take up higher study and practice.

Moved to give back more to others, Yeshe shifted to Chandigarh, a modern city in North India, where he set up a charitable trust to care for sick people from around the Himalayas seeking medical treatment. As the charity became established he started to be approached for teachings and a small group of students grew around him. Student numbers increased as he evolved his teachings to meet the pressing needs of those who came to him. These changes are reflected in the books and teachings he wrote during this time.

Now invited regularly to teach internationally, Yeshe has followers around the world. Attracted by his simple direct teachings that do not promise heavenly realms or mystical experiences but simply allow us to reduce our suffering and the suffering of those around us. In many ways this current book is Buddhism without Buddhism. Yeshe has a knack to communicate the teachings in an unpretentious and clear way. His approach does not require reverence, knowledge of specialist jargon or religious faith. This book instead offers a clear and practical path to lead us in more peaceful and meaningful directions in our lives.

I have given in this brief introduction, more of Yeshe's life than he normally offers up. In his quiet and unassuming way he will be the first to admit that this book or his teachings are not about him at all. It is about the teachings themselves and how they have worked in his life and have practically helped the people around him. That's the important point. As Yeshe often tells people who ask him for advice, "Give it a try, what have you got to lose? "

Stan B. Martin
Author of 'Illusions on the Path'

Part One
Principles

One – Getting Started

Each time I sit down to write this book I get distracted; I get a ping on my phone notifying me that somebody has posted a photo of their lunch on Facebook or a selfie of them standing outside a shopping mall. There are so many distractions in the modern world, some external and some internal. External distractions are easier to control, as we can ditch our phone for a while, sit alone in a room, close our eyes, find a quiet place to re-engage with nature and so on. But internal distractions are far harder to get to grips with. We could be concentrating on something one minute and the next moment wondering what we are going to have for dinner, getting anxious about the future or replaying a situation from the past.

The aim of this book is to help you navigate the choppy waters of your mind. It is not a book that will ask you to 'Think positive and you will be positive' or 'Just visualise what you wish for and you will receive it.' That is just magical thinking. The book will take you on a journey into the deepest regions of your inner life, so you can open your awareness and mind to a lasting peace.

I spent the early part of my life chasing happiness, believing that it was going to set me free. I had great clothes, a big house, expensive cars, ate at the best restaurants and went to the theatre regularly. You may think I was living the dream, but that was all it was, a dream, an illusion. I was dreaming that all these things mattered. It wasn't until I became seriously ill and spent a lot of time on the bed looking up at the ceiling that I realised I was wasting my life. I started to understand that the happiness I had achieved was short lived and was never going to give me the freedom I was searching for. I felt imprisoned by the desires that my mind endlessly came up with. Instead of looking for external happiness, I realised that I should be trying to declutter my mind. I needed to find out how to obtain true peace of mind. All the practices and snippets of advice in this book come from my experience of searching for peace and engaging in Buddhist principles. I hope you will find something here to help you start your own journey towards a more peaceful and uncluttered mind.

The first part of the book explores the workings of your mind and helps you get your mind ready for mindfulness and meditation practices. You can find all the meditations mentioned in this book on the Buddhism Guide Guided Meditation page on Sound Cloud or on The Buddhism Guide app, which is available for free on Google Play or the Apple Store. The second part of the book introduces you to practices that will allow you to change, to grow and become more peaceful. The third section of the book acquaints you with qualities of mind you can cultivate to further reduce your inner suffering and ensure that your mind stays calm and peaceful.

As you move forward you will find various exercises, contemplations, mindfulness practices and meditations. Not all of them will suit you, but please give them a try before you dismiss them. We can only change old patterns by replacing them with new ones. So, a fair amount of effort will be needed, but take that as a challenge and not something to demotivate you.

Honesty is another important part of this journey. It is not about being honest with me or anyone else, but being honest with yourself.

Not only will this journey take effort and honesty, it will also be difficult at times, but I can assure you it is going to be worth it – dare I even suggest, life changing.

Two – Emotional Suffering

What would you say if I told you the largest part of your emotional suffering was caused by yourself? I expect you would be doubtful or even shocked, but it is true. The way we live our lives, our beliefs, biases, concepts and social conditioning all cause us to mentally suffer. By suffering I mean our minds get disturbed, we become disillusioned, dissatisfied, discontented. This often results in stress, anxiety and depression. None of these are helpful or healthy.

The first problem is that our mind never rests, it is always thinking, planning, remembering, organising, it goes on and on. Even when we sit down to relax, our mind carries on working. We can't escape. We become mentally and physically exhausted.

The second problem is, we identify strongly with our self-image, our body, our thoughts, our emotions to the extent that we see them as who we are. We don't see them as just processes of the brain. These experiences cannot be who we are because they are forever changing. We have around 60,000 thoughts a day, so which one is you? Our feelings change from moment to moment, so again, which of your feelings is you? Our emotions are on a roller-coaster, up one minute and down the next, so which emotion do you think is you? Our bodies change moment to moment, so how can we see the body as who we are? Nothing about us is static, we are like a fast-flowing river.

But we don't see ourselves as momentary experiences, we have a solid, singular sense of who we are. So, it is clear that none of these are you. In fact, there is no solid, independent, autonomous you and this is another reason we cause ourselves emotional suffering; we become attached to a deceptive sense of self. However, this so-called self is a mental construct the mind continuously creates in reaction to outside stimulus or thoughts. When there a stimulus or a thought the brain reacts by creating a sense of self to experience it. So, the self is not solid or permanent but fluid. If we are able to see the fluidity of self, then it becomes possible for us to gain some relief from emotional suffering. If you meditate on a regular basis, after some time, you can experience a state of mind that is so peaceful that the mind does not feel the need to construct a self. In that mind, self doesn't arise and there is no sense of a self.

These are important points, so don't carry on reading just yet, pause for some time and contemplate these points one by one. Look at your thoughts, feelings, emotions and your body. Are they permanent? Are they changing moment to moment? Examine your sense of self. Is your sense of self just a mental construct? Can you point to one thing and say, 'This is me'? I doubt you will be able to fully appreciate what is being suggested here straight away, but you can certainly get the ball rolling. It would be wise to keep returning to these points as you travel through this book.

In this book you will find ways to relax the mind, understand the processes of the brain, learn how to find out who you really are and, finally, declutter your mind and find peace. I will also drop in a bit of science from time to time, if I feel it will help make my point. As we all know, there are two types of people; the 'How' people and the 'Why' people. The "How' people will look carefully at the practices and try them out. The 'Why' people will want to know how it works before they give it a go. The science part is for them. I have tried to accommodate both types of people in this book.

****

Here is the first piece of science which looks briefly at our brain, as it is going to be the focus of this book. The brain is divided into two parts, old brain and new brain.

The old brain is all about survival and it determines our most primary emotional reactions. What is interesting here is that this part of the brain has no sense of time. It has absolutely no notion of past, present or future. That is why our emotional pain is often experienced way out of proportion. It feels to us like the hurt has always been this way and always will be. I personally find this point fascinating and I've spent a lot of time contemplating its implications. Of course, I've not come to any earth-shattering realisations, but it does explain why some people are still emotional long after an event has taken place.

The new brain sees our experiences as problems that need to be solved. It tries to make us feel comfortable and safe. It's the part of the brain that observes, analyses, learns, organises and is creative. It also tries to control our experiences and protect us from perceived dangers. In doing so it makes our world view very narrow and small, because we are not seeing things as they are, we are seeing them as we think they are or wish them to be.

One problem we have by allowing the brain to constantly lead us in this way, is that we are always trying to manipulate people and situations to suit our own needs. We may not like to admit this fact, but it is true. However, acting in this way makes us overwhelmed, stressed and anxious. We need to learn to let the world unfold by itself and not try to constantly influence it.

Years ago, scientists believed that the brain stopped changing after adolescence. But due to MRI scans they now know this to be untrue. The brain can change in certain regions all the way up to the moment of death. This is known as Neuroplasticity - the ability to create new connections in the brain. This means our potential is not set at birth and we can constantly strengthen and improve our brains. So, say goodbye to the old saying 'You can't teach an old dog's new tricks.'

Everything we do, or stop doing, has an impact on our brain. It constantly transforms and adapts to the changes in our everyday life. If you stop using a part of the brain it will shrink and if you focus more on another part of the brain it will become stronger. This power to change your brain, is what the exercises and mindfulness meditation practices mentioned in this book will help you develop and achieve in an intentional way. They will assist you in rewiring your brain into a more peaceful and controllable one.

Neurons, which are nerve cells that transmit signals throughout the body, strengthen the more we use them. If we do an action a lot, it creates a superhighway for the neuron to travel down. If we rarely do an action, the path the neuron travels down becomes more like a disused path through a forest. Like water, neurons always want to take the easiest route. So, by consciously doing something we are strengthening the neuron's path and vice versa.

When I was young I had a habit of biting my nails whilst watching films. I would do this unconsciously and only realise it once I had bitten them down so far they began to hurt. I decided to sit on my hands while watching films to stop myself biting my nails. At first, I would forget to sit on my hands and I would end up biting my nails, but slowly, I got in the habit of not biting them. Now my habit is not to bite my nails. This is an example of how I rewired my brain by getting the neurons to take another path. Have you ever rewired your brain without understanding what you are actually doing? Give it some thought, because you most certainly would have.

I am not a scientist, and this is crudely put, but I am sure you will get the point. We have the ability to rewire our brains from old outdated patterns into new, more useful patterns. The idea is what we think, what we do, and most importantly, what we pay attention to, can change our brain. That is what meditation and mindful awareness can do for you. Keep this in mind as you journey through this book – especially when you are starting to lose focus.

****

By following the exercises and meditations in this book, you will be able to cultivate a more spacious sense of awareness, and you can begin to relax into your life and have a more peaceful mind.

I am sure a peaceful mind is what we are all looking for. To have a mind that is relaxed, focused, undisturbed, calm, mindful and contented. The good news is that all of these things are achievable, with a bit of hard work and effort. However, finding the time for this hard work and effort is the real challenge facing most of us. We are all looking for shortcuts and quick fixes. Unfortunately, there are none.

The starting point for this quest is understanding that we have emotional suffering running through our lives. This is no easy task, because we like to fool ourselves into thinking everything is fine and dandy. Whenever we do get glimpses of our emotional suffering we do something like going on a shopping spree to buy back a little piece of happiness. But, if we wish to alleviate our emotional suffering, we need to look inside ourselves and not to the outside world, as that is a fool's game. We buy something and we are usually happy for only a short period of time, but later on when the object breaks, is lost or a newer version comes on the market, it is so easy for our happiness to turn into dissatisfaction. We will never be able to buy our way into lasting happiness and peace of mind. It is like sitting in the sun to cool yourself down.

Whatever we come into contact with through our five senses are experienced by the mind. Whatever thought, feeling and emotion we experience stems from the mind. Any action we do first starts off as a thought in the mind. Your habits, perceptions, concepts and biases all stem from the mind. Any suffering we experience is felt in the mind. Our mind is the way we experience the world. So, if the mind is at peace and free from suffering, we will feel contented, regardless of what we own or what sort of day we are having.

Suffering comes in many forms, so let's look at the different types of suffering we can experience. The first is physical suffering. I think we are all quite aware of this type of suffering. It is a natural process of having a human body. However, we can help to alleviate some of this suffering by eating healthily, exercising and looking after our bodies. This type of suffering is easy for us to understand, as we experience it on a daily basis. I should point out here that this physical suffering can also lead to emotional suffering. Our minds get fixated on the physical pain and can easily, if we are not careful, make it bigger than it actually is. A few years back I had a knee operation and I was told my knee will hurt during the cold, wet, winter months. Of course, the doctor had now planted that seed in my mind and during winter any small pain in my knee was blown all out of proportion by my mind.

The second type is a form of emotional suffering caused by our attachment to happiness. When we are happy we relax and enjoy ourselves. But unfortunately, happiness never lasts and when it changes we begin to mentally suffer. This is very apparent, as I mentioned above, when we try to buy happiness. For example, we get a new car and we are so happy, but a short time later it stops working, is stolen or damaged in an accident and our happiness begins to turn into suffering. This type of suffering is not so easy to understand because we never equate our happiness with future suffering. We get so attached to this notion of being happy that we totally lose sight of the temporary nature of happiness.

The third type of suffering is extremely difficult for us to understand. That is because it a subtle form of emotional suffering. This is caused by the way we think – this is good or bad, this is right or wrong – in other words, it is because we think dualistically and in extremes. If you believe something is good, you get attached to it. If we feel something is bad, we have aversion towards it. Both of these ways of thinking are going to cause you emotional suffering in the end. This type of suffering also stems from the biases we hold, how we try to make situations suit ourselves, how we tend to think emotionally and not rationally, how we overthink situations and experiences, our perceptions and concepts. I could go on, but I think you get the picture. This type of suffering comes about because of our own rigid ways of thinking.

If we want a peaceful mind, we need to acquaint ourselves with these three types of suffering. Don't just quickly move on, reflect on these points for some time and see if you can identify any of these types of suffering in your life.

****

Once we have understood that we have emotional suffering in our lives, and we have become acquainted with the various ways we suffer, the next task is to understand the causes of that suffering. Obviously, there are many possible causes, but I just want to focus on three that are important on this journey of self-discovery.

The first two of the three causes I wish to address are aversion and desire, which are two sides of the same coin.

When we desire things, we tend to cling to them, but with aversion, we do the opposite.

We spend all our time and energy trying to push them away. Aversion drives us to act in negative ways and make adverse comments about things we have a bias against, and a strong feeling of irritation or anger arises within us. However, if we spend time and examine this feeling, we will see it is baseless and irrational. It is through contemplating in this way that we will be able to eventually let the aversion go.

The key to freeing ourselves from the grip of aversion is to acknowledge that we have aversion in the first place. The mind has a knack of fooling us and if we don't recognise it we can quite easily fall into denial, and this is not good for our state of mind.

I had a friend that had an aversion towards dogs. If he saw one, he would either freeze or move quickly in the other direction. I asked him why he was so averse to dogs. He didn't know. He said he had never been bitten by one or even had a bad experience with one. It appeared his aversion was irrational. So, he gave it a lot of thought and realised his aversion came from his mother's dislike of dogs. Slowly he started to be less scared of dogs, and now he is married, he has a dog of his own. So, don't just blindly accept your aversions, check them out and see what the root cause of the aversion is.

Here is a short practice for you to try.

Think of something you have an aversion to, such as a task at home, shopping, talking to someone on the phone or office work.

This week, try to be as present as possible during the task, performing it slowly and mindfully, and notice how this feels and how groundless the aversion is.

Desire is like an itch, once we start scratching it is difficult to stop. Once we have something new, we start wanting something else. This is because we wrongly believe that material things can make us truly happy. However, if we investigate, we will find that our desires eventually lead us into a feeling of discontentment and dissatisfaction. There is no problem in desiring things and trying to make our lives more comfortable; the problem is clinging and grasping at these desires. We get attached to things and when they break, are stolen or die – which they inevitably will – we become discontented and unhappy.

Our desires lead us to act in certain ways, such as being proud, jealous and protective, and this in turn leads to our discontentment. Desire leads to action, which in turn leads to discontentment. Desire, action and discontentment are like an endlessly rotating wheel. To break this cycle we have to understand that constantly chasing our desires leads us away from satisfaction and peace of mind.

Of course, not all desire is unhealthy. We may have a selfless desire to help others. This is a worthwhile desire and is not likely to bring you any emotional suffering. The desire I am talking about here is the selfish, grasping type of desire. The desire that leads you to spend money you don't have or buy things solely to impress others. Do you think this type of desire is ever going to bring you fulfilment?

Pause here a moment and think over the following: bring to mind something you bought recently. Something you had been craving for. Once you had it for some time, did it still bring you the same amount of happiness as when you first obtained it? Has it lost its sparkle? Are you now craving for something different?

The next cause that leads to emotional suffering is anger, aggression and hatred. These can be extremely destructive emotions because they take control of us. Many people in the West say anger is natural and should be expressed at all costs. I believe expressing or repressing are both unhelpful and dangerous for all concerned.

When we express it, it can lead to fights, arguments and people's feelings being hurt. Also, the more you let your anger out the more it becomes a habit and we all know just how hard habits are to break. If you repress it, you are just storing up trouble for the future.

You may be able to keep it down for some time, but eventually it will surface and may even come back stronger.

If we observe our angry feelings, we will see that they stem from either exaggerating the negative qualities of someone, or projecting negative qualities that are not actually there onto someone or something.

There is no doubt that anger creates problems for us and the person we are angry with, so here are two antidotes to anger – of course, you may have your own tried and tested antidotes.

Cultivate patience by not reacting straight away but take a deep breath or count to ten. This will give you the space to reflect on the situation and help you calm down and see things more rationally. My mother used to tell me to count to ten, but by that time I was already being controlled by anger and so couldn't think properly. That is why we should be trying to catch the anger before it takes hold. So, until you have managed to become a more patient person, I would suggest simply walking away until you have calmed down.

Analysing is another way to help with your anger issues. Of course, this can only be done once the anger has begun to subside. Sit quietly, close your eyes and look closely at your anger, you will see that it is built on exaggeration and negative projections. Look at actual situations where you have become angry, and their outcome. Bring up the emotions you felt at that time. Think about what the consequences were. Sit with those feelings for a while. Now think about how you could have reacted without losing your temper. Sit with those feelings. You can see that your emotions are in turmoil when you are angry, and this is not a good state of mind to make any decisions.

As I said, there are numerous causes of emotional suffering in our lives. I have introduced three that are important. I encourage you to look at which of these three brings you the most emotional suffering and then work on that first.

Three - Developing Redlines

At different times in my life I have found myself adrift at sea. I unintentionally upset people or found myself in tight spots. This was because I hadn't set myself any boundaries. I hadn't worked out any redlines. I was just allowing myself to be blown around aimlessly.

Boundaries are the imaginary redlines we draw around ourselves to keep our bodies, minds, emotions and behaviour in balance. They provide a framework of values that prevent us causing harm to ourselves or others. An essential part of being a human, having redlines drawn allow us to live peacefully and responsibly within our communities. Knowing the redlines we are not willing to cross is an important part of establishing our identity, as well as being crucial for our mental health and well-being. So, clearly setting out and being mindful of our redlines allows us to live each moment, fully aware that we are not going to unknowingly cause any harm. They put us firmly into the driver's seat of our lives.

There are different types of redlines, such as those that define the physical way we act, the thoughts we allow, and the way we communicate with others. I am not only talking about the redlines society has drawn for us, such as not killing, not stealing, not lying. We also need to examine the individual redlines we set for ourselves. Society says drinking alcohol responsibly is ok, that doesn't work for me, so not drinking alcohol is a personal redline I draw. Society says having sex, as long as it is not harming someone, is ok, but I am a monk, so sex is a redline for me. We are unique individuals so the redlines we draw need to be relevant to the unique circumstances we each live in. Your redlines should reflect your character, so they may differ from what society tells you is good and bad. I am not saying don't keep within society's redlines, of course we must, as we are social beings, but we must also work out our own particular needs. Our redlines are not set in stone and as we grow and change, so will they. Don't make them so rigid that they are impossible to keep, or so loose that they simply don't work. Try to find the middle path between these two extremes.

Below I have mentioned some examples of redlines that will help keep us on the right track. To start with, I always think a great rule-of-thumb is if you would not like it to happen to you, then it's a safe bet nobody else will like it either. Now, these are only suggestions and not a set of commandments. In the end, you are going to have to set your own redlines, but first, let's look at some suggestions.

Non-harming

I think most people would agree that we should try our best not to harm others. For me, the concept of harm extends beyond humans and also includes animals, plants, flowers, trees and, most importantly, the planet. This is my personal choice. Extending redlines in these areas works for me. I believe treating people disrespectfully, needlessly cutting flowers or chopping down trees, eating meat and dairy, encroaching on wild animal's habitat, polluting the environment and so on, are all acts that harm others. We are intimately connected and everything we do has effects that reverberate outwards into the world. I am not saying this to be pious or self-righteous, I am saying it because harmful actions have a tendency to come back and bite us. If I go around being violent to others or killing things, how am I ever going to find peace of mind?

A mind free from violence is the skilful way to live in the world. By this I mean, we should not even have a single thought to harm others. It is not that we should stop ourselves from harming, we should not even have the thought in the first place. This takes practice but is achievable.

Taking what has not been given

Respecting other people's possessions is another redline to draw and adhere to. We live in a world where greed and desire are celebrated, but if we want peace of mind, we need to learn to be contented and grateful for what we have. Many people may have more things than us, but this need not produce envy or desire in us. Acting in a contented and generous way is the best strategy – instead of taking, give.

Communication

It is always helpful to keep a check on how we communicate with others. It seems these days people think they can write or say any vile thing that pops into their heads. Social media has brought out the worst in people. When I published my second book, which was secular Buddhist in nature, I received a torrent of abuse. People questioned why I was a monk and if I just wore the robes to make money. I got a lot of cruel comments that I could not even repeat here. Some may say it's my own fault, because if you put your head above the parapet you are going to be shot at. In some respects that is true but doesn't give others a free license to abuse anyone.

The main worry here is that abuse is starting to become the new norm. It certainly doesn't help when politicians and others in authority feel they are free to tweet whatever they feel. So, we need to think before we speak to others or when we post something on social media. Another aspect to be aware of is the fake news we spread and consume online. We used to call it 'lying.' We need to ensure our words and what we communicate is true and factual. If we mislead people, we end up harming them and ourselves. We will get a reputation for being a liar and people simply will not trust us.

Truthfulness

We should always try to be straightforward and truthful, even if it is uncomfortable for us. I think there is a caveat here. I believe we need to split this aspect into two; what is appropriate and what is inappropriate. Sometimes, what we are about to say may be true, but it is going to cause untold harm to another, and this is where we should apply caution. We need to ask ourselves what the most appropriate course of action is. It's a tricky one, but if you have the other person's welfare in mind, and not just your own, you shouldn't go far wrong.

Divisive speech

This is when we say things that are going to cause a rift between two or more people. This type of speech is found quite a lot in the workplace or social gatherings. Many years ago, I worked in the hospitality industry and I found the workers split themselves into divisive groups. There were waiting staff who used to talk badly about the chefs. The chefs spoke badly about the front of house staff. They spoke badly about managers and managers spoke badly about everyone. It was such a divisive atmosphere. It caused many unnecessary problems and infighting. The skilful approach to this is kind words that draw people together and not push them apart.

Harsh words

Swear-words, bad language or words that are said to cause harm, bring untold pain. They are never useful or kind, and usually stem from anger or impatience. This is where we really do need to be mindful, because if we aren't, we may find ourselves regretting what we have said and apologising each time we hurt people with harsh words. If we act in a skilful way, our words will be pleasant and constructive.

Gossiping

This type of speech can also be hurtful. Now, I have been told on many occasions that there is nothing wrong with a bit of gossip. I expect they are saying that because they are doing the gossiping. I wonder how they would feel if they were the topic of some hot gossip? I am sure they wouldn't like it. So, there is no doubt that gossiping is not only unkind and unhelpful, it is also a waste of time and is disturbing to our minds. The skilful way to act is to ensure your words are helpful and encouraging. We all like to have a good chat over a cup of coffee, but we have to ensure we are not bringing harm to anyone while indulging in idle talk.

Many years ago I was the subject of some hot gossip. I had been ill and taken some time off work. When I returned it soon became apparent that people thought I had been on holiday and had faked my sickness. I was the boss at the time and this gossip started to erode my authority. There was a bad atmosphere for several weeks and I felt hurt and let down. I can still vividly recollect this incident to this very day.

We all understand the power of *words*. *Words* shape our perception of the world; *words* trigger emotions; *words* wound; *words* have consequences. So, the redlines we set defining how we communicate with others are extremely important, if we cannot learn to control our words, how are we going to try and take back control of our minds?

Sexual Behaviour

How we relate with others sexually is also an area we should examine. Behaviours that can lead to violence, rape, underage sex or forcing a partner to do something they are not comfortable with. Also, we need to respect other people's sexuality and choices - as long as they are not harming others. I am thinking about gay, lesbian, trans-sexual and trans-gender people. We may not understand their choices, but we should respect and have compassion for them.

The skilful aspect of this is self-regulation. We need self-regulation in all aspects of our lives, but particularly where sexual behaviour is concerned. Notice I used self-regulation and not self-control. There is a good reason for that. I believe self-control is about trying to suppress your actions. We are dealing with the situation by stopping ourselves acting in a way we want to, because we think it is not acceptable. Whereas, people with self-regulation use creativity and empathy to consider alternative avenues that can help them accomplish their goals. So, they decide on an action, they consider their own feelings and concerns, but they are also empathetic and consider other people's perspectives as well. This is what is needed here.

Intoxicants

While setting our redlines, we should try to avoid substances that alter our minds, such as alcohol and illegal drugs. It is difficult to rein our minds in at the best of times, but when we are drunk or high, it is impossible. I am not saying everyone should stop drinking alcohol, we have to make our own choices. However, what I am saying is that once we lose control of our minds, we start to lose control of our boundaries, ethics and values. My advice is, 'Everything in moderation,' as long as it is not illegal or harming yourself or others.

Limiting our desires

Another useful redline for us to try and follow is not blindly chasing after our desires. A lot of the time our desires are being led by greed or wanting what other people possess. We see they have something, and we start to crave it. This can lead to pride, jealousy and, in some cases, theft or violence. So, covetousness is an unskilful act and a redline we should try not to cross. Contentment is the skilful way to act. If we feel we have everything we require, we will not be constantly looking to see what others have. We will understand the difference between need and greed.

Creating safe space

The final redline I wish to discuss here is animosity towards others. This is when we have ill-will, hostility, malice or resentment towards a person or a group of people. This animosity may only be in our head, but thoughts lead to actions, so even having unpleasant thoughts and feelings towards someone is not going to be helpful. Having kind, supportive, friendly thoughts is a great way to be, as this leads to a willingness to be empathetic and compassionate. If an ill feeling does arise in your mind, don't act upon it. Instead, look at why you are feeling that way, what is the root cause of your hostility. This will help you let the ill feeling go without having to act upon it.

Drawing redlines have helped me throughout my life, and I constantly reflect on them. You will have your own set to follow, I just expressed these to give you an idea of some that may be helpful to you. The important thing is to keep our redlines at the forefront of our minds. We will then start to reduce some of our emotional suffering and start our journey towards feeling peaceful. From time to time it is inevitable that we will fall short. We shouldn't feel guilty or become tormented, because we are only human. When we do cross our personal redlines, we should just reaffirm our commitment to them, learn from the experience and move on.

Before the next section, I want you to sit and contemplate your core values. I have mentioned mine here, but what are yours?

It is extremely important for you to understand where you wish to draw your redlines. Once you know, you will be able to align your actions of body, speech and mind with what you most value in life. This is an extremely powerful combination and essential for finding peace of mind.

Four - Unhelpful Interruptions

I would love to tell you that this journey into the far reaches of your mind is going to be plain sailing, but unfortunately, I can't. There are going to be obstacles and hindrances along the way, which, if left unchecked, could obstruct and impede your progress. I will briefly introduce some common negative mental states that I have encountered and suggest ways to counter them. As always, your inner journey will be a personal affair and you will of course encounter different obstacles. Below is just a selection of the common ones.

Desires of the senses

This is a big distraction in everyone's lives. In fact, sensual desires can consume our whole thought process if we are not vigilant. The greatest part of our day is consumed by what we see, hear, smell, taste or touch. We get bounced around like a ping-pong ball from one sense object to another.

This hindrance is activated when our senses come into contact with sense objects, our minds become fascinated and we start telling ourselves stories about how wonderful the object is, how we really need it and it's the one thing that is going to make us happy. We get stupefied by these sense objects and begin to crave and get attached to them.

The antidote to this is to think about the impermanent nature of the objects. If things are compounded, that is to say, made up of two or more things, they are by their very nature impermanent. The parts come together, last for a period of time and then break up. If we contemplate this we can clearly see this in our interactions with our friends and family, with our belongings and even with our own bodies.

If you are consumed by desires, look at what is making you dissatisfied. Why are you always wanting new things? Is it peer pressure, unhappiness with your life, greed, discontentment or are you simply a shopaholic? It is only when we have discovered the root of these desires that we can start to change.

Of course, not all desires are unwelcome. The desire to make changes in our lives or the desire to help people are positive desires. The problem is those desires that lead to attachment and eventually disappointment.

I remember when I lived in the UK and a new Range Rover was released. I loved it and every time I saw one I got a rush of adrenaline. I simply had to have one. Luckily, I could afford it, but as I lived in the centre of London I certainly didn't need a four-wheel drive SUV. The day I collected it from the dealership I drove around London feeling like the king of the world. I decided to stop at a coffee shop and show my friend my new toy. While I was inside someone knocked the door mirror off. In the space of two hours my excitement had turned to anger, sadness and frustration. I learned a valuable lesson that day; the happiness that comes from satisfying our sense desires is extremely short lived and will eventually lead us into some form of suffering.

Hostility towards others

Another obstacle I am sure we will encounter is ill-will, which is to have angry, unkind or destructive thoughts about some other person, though it is also possible to have ill-will towards a situation or even towards ourselves. It can make you burn inside and consume you so much that you are unable to concentrate on anything else but your destructive emotions. It is usually driven by resentment, jealousy, pride or anger.

In my early years, I had a lot of ill-will towards others, especially those who were outgoing and good in social situations. I was shy and just couldn't bring myself to talk to strangers. It left me with extremely bitter feelings and disturbed my mind so much. I eventually understood that having ill-will towards them was not going to solve my problem, in fact, it was just making it worse.

There is no doubt that this is an extremely powerful hindrance, and the antidote is to develop compassion towards others. The reason we have ill-will is because we see other people as different from us, as outside of us. We do not see how we are interconnected. We need to see that everyone is in a similar situation, even the animals around us. We all strive for peace in our lives and we all wish to escape pain and suffering. If we see that others are no different from us in this sense, we will start to build compassion towards them, or at the very least we will be empathic towards them. This practice will help to reduce ill-will and hostility.

Lack of enthusiasm

We all get moments of apathy and laziness, which makes our mind numb. It becomes virtually impossible for us to concentrate. Apathy makes it difficult for us to arouse any interest in anything of value while laziness makes us lethargic and sleepy. They both make it very difficult for us to bring about change in our lives.

If we feel this way we need to ask ourselves, what is making us lazy and disinterested? Is it boredom, are we unwell? Perhaps we do not understand what we are supposed to be doing or are we just not seeing any benefit from the things that we are doing? We have to give it a lot of thought and get right into the causes of our apathy and laziness.

Emotional strain

Anxiety, stress and tension are very prominent hindrances these days. It could be that we are stressed from work or even from the journey home. We may have money problems, be worried about the future. Our mind may just be overloaded. This hindrance makes us overexcited and emotionally troubled. We can lose our ability to concentrate on anything for any length of time. This is because we are not living in the present moment. Our thoughts are either in the past or the future.

The antidote, which will bring you into the present moment, is to take three slow, deep breaths in through the nose, hold for a few seconds and then blow all the air out through your mouth. This will bring in much needed oxygen into the body, make your mind calm and body relaxed and put you in a better frame of mind to continue.

If you are a person who is anxious about everything, find out why. Is it work, relationships, illness, lack of money, loneliness or depression? Dig deep and find what makes you anxious. If it is severe anxiety, I would advise you to seek medical advice. Whatever you do, do not ignore it. Your anxiety will not miraculously disappear on its own.

Lack of confidence

Doubt is another obstacle, which occurs when we lack confidence or understanding. It could be we don't comprehend what we should be doing, we don't trust that it will work or we think we are not capable of doing it correctly. All of these make us wonder if what we are doing is benefiting us.

The most simple and effective way to clear up doubt is to ask questions, read books or surf the Internet for answers (be careful here as the net is full of misinformation). Sometimes, doubt is looked upon as a very unhelpful thing. We are often asked to just believe what we are taught. I find that attitude extremely unhelpful. I have always asked lots of questions if I do not understand something, and it has always cleared away my doubt.

When I was studying Buddhist Philosophy in a Monastery in Nepal the teacher stated that only men can become enlightened, of course that set off alarm bells in my head. I instantly had doubts. I put my hand up to ask him to clarify and he refused. Later when the students were all talking in the canteen everyone had massive doubts. Because the teacher wouldn't clear up these doubts many questions were left unanswered, and I have to say the teacher lost a lot of respect that day. Remember, doubts left unresolved fester and grow.

Look at the doubts you carry around with you. Find out where the doubt is in your life. See how it is affecting your life and holding you back. Don't see your doubt as a negative thing. See it as a way for you to change and grow.

These are just some examples of obstacles you may run up against while you look deeply into your mind. We have to understand that these hindrances are mental states and, as such, stem from our minds. So, it is no good trying to blame anyone else. We may think it is another person's fault that we have ill-will, we might blame work for making us anxious or think that it's the teacher's fault that we have doubts. All of these are wrong views. It is our minds that   generates the hindrances, and so it is our responsibility to deal with them.

Part Two

Practices

Five - Reflective Practice

Part one has been laying the groundwork for the rest of the book. In part two we will be looking at various practices and the best way to approach them. I believe there are three aspects of a daily practice, namely meditation, mindfulness and reflection.

I want to start by introducing you to a daily reflective practice. A great deal of our actions of body, speech and mind are carried out unconsciously. This is because we have done the action so many times in the past it has become a habit. This process is good for helpful actions, but totally counterproductive for harmful ones. So, to evaluate the direction our actions are taking us, I recommend a daily reflective session to look back over the key experiences of the day – both helpful and harmful and try to see where changes are required.

Reflecting is a way for us to examine ourselves, to gain insight into our experience of life. Everyone's reality is different and stems from his or her own mind. To be able to reflect our mind has to be calm, stable and focused. It is impossible to see into a bucket of muddy water when it has been stirred up. But if you allow the water to settle, the mud will fall to the bottom and the water will become clearer. The same happens with our mind. If it is agitated, you will not be able to gain any insight; but if it is calm, stable and focused, you will be able to gain the insight you require. So, by sitting quietly and looking back over our day, we will be allowing the mud to settle in our mind and we can then start to look back objectively.

What do we wish to gain from a reflection practice? I believe it is threefold, namely a sense of emotional awareness, self-evaluation and self-confidence.

By building a strong emotional awareness you develop clarity into your own emotions and emotional processes. In time, you gain the ability to objectively perceive your emotions as they arise and accept them, both pleasant and unpleasant. This objectivity is essential for the next step, self-awareness. This arises when we are able to be honest with ourselves about our own strengths and weaknesses. We are clear about who we are and what our values are. We begin to be comfortable in our own skin, and that creates the conditions for self-confidence.

As we become more regular with our daily reflection practice we develop emotional awareness, which means we begin to see the emotions behind our actions, such as pride, jealousy, anger and so on. This awareness improves our capacity for self-evaluation. We can see more objectively what worked for us and what didn't. It shows us clearly where changes need to be made, emotionally, psychologically and physically. When we become better at self-evaluation we will naturally become more self-confident.

We can achieve emotional awareness, self-evaluation and self-confidence by doing the following daily reflective practice.

To calm your mind ready for this practice I suggest you sit somewhere quiet and lightly close your eyes. Now bring your awareness to your breath. Breathe in through your nose to the count of 5, hold the breath to the count of 6 and then slowly let the air out through your mouth to the count of 7. Do these three times and you should be ready to reflect. If you are still not focused, do some more 5-6-7 breaths until you feel calm.

Now look at the actions that worked for you today, this allows you to reinforce them and makes it easier to do the same action in the future. Then look back over the actions that didn't work for you (remember, this includes all acts stemming from body, speech and mind). This practice allows you to examine why it didn't work and reframe the act into something more positive. This can be done by rehearsing a better way to act, so in future you will naturally act in a more constructive way.

Also, while reflecting, look at the emotions behind your act, what feelings arose, examine any sensations in your body and try to find the *reason you acted in such a way. It could be because of ego, past patterns or tiredness. The more you understand the reasoning, the more you become self-aware.*

Remember, we are not trying to beat ourselves up over the way we acted, we are simply trying to change what didn't work.

We are constantly told that we learn from our experiences, but this obviously is not true, because if it were, we would never make the same mistake twice, but we do. In truth, we learn from reflecting on our experiences. This is why the daily reflective practice is so powerful.

I will be coming back to the daily reflective practice throughout this book, because it is a big part of the change we need to bring about, in order to produce more peace in our lives.

Remember, change will not come by simply reading this book. You must put what you learn into practice. That way you will experience change for yourself, and that, to me, is the only way.

I have to say that some of the biggest changes I have made in my life came about through reflection. That is why I try to encourage all my students to start a regular reflection practice. Even today, if I have an experience that disturbed my mind, or I found myself in an unfavourable situation, I always revert to doing a reflection practice. I feel it gives me the time and space to work things out.

So, before you move on, try a reflective practice – it doesn't matter what time of day it is, this is just a dummy run to give you some experience of what I am talking about.

Six - Mindful Awareness

I am sure we have all experienced our mind suddenly wandering off to the past or leaping forward to the future. Usually at the most inopportune moments. I know I do on a regular basis. So, how do we go about reining the mind in? Mindful awareness is the answer, it is a great way of helping us bring the mind back under our control. The next question is, 'Do we need to rein it in?' I think most definitely the answer is yes. A mind left to wander can be a disruptive and destructive thing.

You could liken mindful awareness to a leash on a guide dog. A visually impaired person has their guide dog on a leash, so it keeps the dog walking by their side. Wherever the person goes, the guide dog goes. They work together, and they help each other. But if you take that leash off the dog would just go wandering about wherever it wanted to, which would be of no use to the visually impaired person. The same is the case with our mind. If we don't put a leash on our mind it will start to wander off and just go wherever it wants to and it will invariably disturb us. So, by putting a leash on our mind means it is then working with us, helping us. So, in this analogy, the leash I'm talking about is mindful awareness. If you're being mindful, then you and your mind are working together. If you're not mindful, your mind is liable to just shoot off in whichever direction it wants to go in.

If we were being honest with ourselves, we would see that we spend most of our waking hours fixating on the past or dreaming about the future. We relive painful experiences from our past or construct elaborate scenarios of what we think may happen in the future – but, in my experience, very rarely does. This brings us untold emotional suffering because we never stop to check our thoughts, feelings or emotions. We just blindly follow them.

This ability to plan for the future and to have memories from the past really is a double-edged sword. it is a blessing and it's also a curse. It's a blessing because we can plan our life; we can plan ahead. So, it's a blessing in that way. Other animals do not have this ability, they just react to whatever comes in front of them. A dog doesn't wake up in the morning and think at 12 o'clock I will bite someone. A person walks by the dog and he bites them. There is no planning involved.

But this ability can also be a curse because we spend so much of our day looking to the future and missing what is happening now, right in this moment. We can think two hours, three hours, one day, one month, one year ahead. People even do five-year plans. How do they know where they are going to be in five years? How do they even know where they are going to be in five minutes time? Will they even be alive? So, in that respect, it's a curse because it constantly takes us into the future, which, in all honesty, is just a figment of our imagination.

Our memories can also be a blessing if we are recalling happier times but can be a curse if we are recollecting unhappy times.

This ability to think about the past or the future can make us act out of habit or in a way we end up regretting later. We do not need to blindly follow every thought, but sadly we do. If you throw a stick for a dog it will run after it without giving it any thought. We are the same, the mind throws up a thought and we run after it without giving it a second thought. By obsessing over the past and future we are emotionally torturing ourselves.

When we stop trudging back to the past or flitting off to the future, we become present in the moment. We start to pay attention to what is happening right now. We become aware of what thoughts are arising, what we are feeling, what emotions are present, what sensations we feel in the body. We start to engage with our immediate environment and become aware of what actions we are taking. It allows us to move from the unconscious to the conscious mind and get a full moment-by-moment experience. This helps to calm and steady the mind, giving us the space to see which thoughts we should follow, and which we should drop like a hot potato.

When we are being mindful we are looking at our mind in a non-judgemental way. We are just observing with equanimity, we are not trying to control or suppress our thoughts, feelings and emotions, but remain present with them, whether they happen to be pleasant or unpleasant. This gives us the chance to reflect before we act. Remember, mindful awareness is not going to make your life perfect – that is just wishful thinking. Unsavoury things will still happen to you, that is life, but you will be able to face them better, and make better conscious decisions, which will stop you blindly following unhelpful, outdated patterns.

Mindful awareness allows us to look at what is arising in an open, friendly and more compassionate way. It gives us a choice, act or don't act. If what is arising is helpful, we should act upon it. However, if it is unskilful and harmful, we should not act and just let the thought go – don't worry, another thought will be coming right behind. In this way we will be acting from the conscious mind and not reacting from the unconscious mind.

For example, maybe you get angry easily and when someone shouts you automatically shout back. This is reacting from your unconscious mind. If you were being mindful, you would not blindly react but think about what the best course of action in this situation. You can then decide to shout or not shout. Mindful awareness is giving you a choice – react in an unconscious way or respond in a conscious way.

When our mind is agitated it is impossible for us to think clearly, but when we allow the mind to settle we can start to focus again. We can see just what is present, be it anger, pride, fear, jealousy, happiness, excitement and so on. This insight gives us choices. We no longer need to follow whatever comes into our mind. We understand that thoughts are just thoughts, not facts, and we can decide on the most skilful way to act. This will help reduce our emotional suffering and that of those around us.

So, we are training our attention in a way that we can create a quality of mind that is calm and clear on-demand – the key word here is on-demand. Imagine people are getting angry with you and you are able to create a mind that is calm and clear, one that has conscious choices. That is a truly liberating experience.

You may think this sounds wonderful, but impossible to do. Well, it's not.

Do this little experiment – sit quietly with your eyes lightly closed. Now, become aware of the sensation as your breath flows into and out of your nose. Watch every aspect of the breath; watch it entering, watch the pause and watch the air leaving. Give it your full attention and if your mind wanders, just gently bring it back to watching the breath again. Now, just become aware of how you are feeling at the moment. Don't judge or try to change it, just experience the feeling. Now, look at your thoughts in the same way. Finally, become aware of your emotions.

Congratulations, you have just been mindful. You weren't thinking about the past or the future, but just being present in the moment. Of course, mindful awareness takes practice, but like everything else, the more we do it the easier it becomes.

A note of caution here; because we have the ability to imagine the future and remember the past, we can never be 100% mindful. We need to constantly bring ourselves back to the present moment. So, in this respect it is a journey and not a destination.

To begin practicing mindful awareness, we should start small. Every now and again, take a calming breath, engage your senses – what can you hear, smell, taste, see, touch, look around you at the environment, look inside you at your thoughts, feelings, emotions and body sensations. Try to do that without adding or taking something away, just observe and become aware. Simply allow your awareness to be attentive without interpretation.

You can begin to incorporate more acts from your daily routine as you become more experienced. Try cleaning your teeth, showering, walking, eating and so on in a mindful way. That means using all of your senses and becoming fully aware of the task you are doing. Try not to let your thoughts go off to the future or slip back to the past. If they do, just re-engage with the present moment.

Let me address some questions I get asked a lot, the first is, "What do we need to be mindful of?" The answer is, everything. We must be mindful of our actions and the impact they have on ourselves and others. These actions will shape our lives now and in the future, so it is important to keep bringing yourself back to the present moment.

We must be aware of our speech, of what we are saying, how we are saying it and to whom. We have to be mindful of our body actions and again, be aware of their impact. Be mindful of our thoughts, feelings and emotions. We also need to be mindful of the work we do and its impact on society. We need to be mindful of the effort we are putting into ensuring all our actions of body, speech and mind are in line with living responsibly. And most importantly, we need to be aware of other people around us. Engage with them in a mindful way by being empathic and compassionate.

Secondly, I get asked these questions, "This all sounds great. So, why do we have difficulty being in the here and now? What gets in the way of our being mindful? What are the obstacles to being present in the moment?" The answer to all of these is our mind. It is forever chattering, distracting us and telling us stories.

We tend to separate ourselves from the present by narrating our experience as it's happening. We essentially follow ourselves around, ceaselessly commenting on our own experience. 'Oh wow, I'm having a good time here,' 'This is going well,' 'They seem to like me,' 'I'm good at this' and so on. This is the soundtrack to our life.

Thoughts are the way the mind tries to manage the present moment. It tries to control and make sense of our present experience, in the hope of steering the present in a direction it wishes to go in. Truthfully, the present moment doesn't need the mind to make it happen; it is unfolding without the mind's help.

There is a story, I don't know if it is true or not, it doesn't really matter as it explains mindful awareness perfectly. A man asked Buddha, "What do you and your monks' practice?" And Buddha said, "Walking, eating, sitting, talking." The man was surprised and said, "We all walk and eat and sit and talk." Buddha replied, "Yes, but when we're walking, we know we're walking. When we're talking, we know we're talking. When we're eating, we know we're eating. When we're sitting, we know we're sitting." I think that's such a good story because it really says what mindfulness is all about. It's not about doing anything special. It's not about doing anything extraordinary or anything mystical or magical. It's about doing the everyday things but being present and knowing that we're doing these things. We all walk, we all talk, we all eat, we all rest. We do all of these things on a daily basis, but do we know we're doing them? When you're eating, are you fully aware that you're eating or are you eating and looking at your mobile phone or watching the television or talking to somebody?

When you're walking, are you fully aware that you're walking or are you looking around judging, criticising or comparing? You may pass somebody in the street, you know nothing about their history, you've never seen them before, but instantly you look at the way they're walking, their hair, their clothes and you instantly judge them. They are just stories that your mind is telling you. That is because you're allowing your mind to just go free. You've taken the leash off the mind and you've just let it wander off.

So, mindfulness just means whatever we're doing, the ordinary, everyday things we're doing, we're doing them with a sense of awareness. We're doing them in an open and focused way.

****

Before we move on here are a few daily mindful awareness practices you may like to try.

- Try to focus on your breathing throughout the day. Become aware of the breath flowing into the nose and flowing back out again, as this will gently bring you back to the moment.
- Do daily routines mindfully, such as walking, talking, washing, cleaning teeth, driving and so on. An excellent practice to fit into your daily routine is mindful eating. A meal usually takes around 10 to 15 minutes and in that time, we should focus all of our awareness on the food – what it looks like, where it came from and its taste. What usually happens these days is we add another task to meal times, such as gossiping, reading, listening to music, checking social media. So, next time you

have a meal, eat it with mindful awareness.

- Actively engage in mindful speaking and listening. A lot of the time we are not actively listening to the person in front of us. They are speaking and we have already decided what they are going to say, and we are starting to rehearse our response. This means we have stopped listening. This means we could quite easily miss what the person is really trying to say. So wait until they have finished speaking before you form a response – a response only takes one sixth of a second. When you talk, ensure you talk mindfully, which means your words are well chosen, so as not to cause any harm or misunderstanding.

- If you are feeling stressed, anxious, depressed and so on, take a mindful S.N.A.C.K.

> **S**top and take a moment to fully focus your awareness.

➤ **N**otice what is happening inside and out.

➤ **A**ccept and acknowledge whatever is troubling you – don't fight it.

➤ **C**urious – look closely at what you are feeling and think about what you need right now to help you through this difficult time.

➤ **K**indness – be kind and supportive of yourself. If you have made a mistake don't berate yourself, understand that you are human and not a machine. Learn from the mistake and then help yourself move on. If someone else has hurt you, understand that they are also human and prone to mistakes. Forgive them and move one.

- Do a mindful one-minute scan throughout the day – body, thoughts and emotions. Stop what you are doing and lightly close your eyes. Now observe your thoughts, are they positive or negative (remember, we are observing and not judging here). Now look at your emotions, what is the predominant emotion you are feeling at the moment. Finally, observe your body, what sensations can you feel. This exercise will bring you back to the present moment, where you can begin to respond to whatever is going on.
- Mindful awareness is all about bringing yourself back to the present moment, so put little reminders in key places, such as your desk, computer, fridge or anywhere you visit frequently. The note can simply say 'Breathe.'
- If you notice strong emotions arising do a short breathing exercise, such as S.T.O.P.

  ➢ **S**top what you are doing for a moment, find a quiet place and sit down.

➢ **T**ake three deep calming breaths. Focus your awareness on your breath and breathe in slowly and deeply through your nose. Hold the breath and then push all the air out through your mouth.

➢ **O**bserve your thoughts, feelings, emotions and your environment. Don't judge them, just become aware of them. Think of the best way to help yourself through this difficult time: read a book, go for a walk, have a cup of tea, take a break – whatever works for you.

➢ **P**roceed with what you were doing, but this time do it with a mind that is open, clear and focused.

The STOP practice can also be used to observe with your mind, your body or your surroundings.

● Use your senses to bring yourself present in the moment. Look around at your surroundings, listen to what sounds you can hear, smell the air and see what different smells there are, feel your clothes touching your body or your feet touching the floor. As with all these daily mindful awareness practices, they have to be observed and not judged or criticised.

- If you feel stressed, anxious or overwhelmed, your mind is most likely fixating on the past or the future. One of the best ways. To bring yourself back into the present moment and calm yourself down is to adjust your breathing. One excellent technique to try is to breathe six times a minute: each breath five seconds in, five seconds out. Consciously slowing down your breathing in this way for about one or two minutes brings you into a much more calm and peaceful state of mind.

To finish this chapter, I want to explain how mindful breathing practices work. Breathing in a mindful way from the abdomen you stimulate the vagus nerve, which runs from the neck down to the abdomen and is said to play a key function in maintaining the mind-body connection. Stimulating this nerve activates your relaxation response, reducing your heart rate and blood pressure. Doing the six breaths per minute practice, or any other mindful abdominal breathing exercise, will stimulate the vagus nerve enough to allow it to stop the stress response.

The vagus nerve responds to your breathing and sends messages to the brain. The brain in turn sends a message to the heart, which adapts the heart rate in response. Whenever we breathe in, sensory nodes in our lungs transmit information up through the vagus nerve and into the brain, and when we breathe out, the brain sends information back down through the vagus nerve to slow down or speed up the heart. So, when we breathe quickly, our heart speeds up, and we feel stressed, anxious, fearful and overwhelmed. Conversely, when we breathe slowly, the heart slows and we become calm, relaxed, focused and more in control.

Seven - Anchoring Your Breath

Before we look at a practice that will become the very foundation of all your meditation practices, I want to expand upon what I see as the science behind meditation.

There are four major categories of brain waves, which correspond to different activities. Meditation enables us to move from higher frequency brain waves to lower frequency, which activates different parts of the brain. When our brain waves are slower there is more time between thoughts. This allows us to skilfully choose which thoughts to follow and what actions to take.

Here is a brief description of the four categories of brain waves:

Beta State – this is the state we spend most of our day in. It is associated with the thinking mind.

Alpha State – brain waves start to slow down, and we feel calm, peaceful and grounded. This is the state we can achieve after just a few sessions of meditation.

Theta State - This is the point where the verbal/thinking mind switches to the meditative/visual mind. We begin to move from the planning mind to a deeper state of awareness. This state is achieved after meditating regularly for some time.

Delta State – people who have been meditating for decades can reach this state. However, we also reach this state during deep, dreamless sleep.

When we begin regular meditation we quickly start to enter the Alpha state. Then after a few months we start to experience the Theta state. If we continue to meditate regularly for a longer period, we enter the Delta state. In this state we do not have a sense of self and so we have no clinging, attachment or desire for anything. Our mind is at complete rest.

On a normal, average sort of day, we stay in the Beta state and when we go to bed at night we to go to the Delta state. If these four states were gears on our car, it would mean we spend the greater part of our lives in 1st and 4th gear. Imagine what that would do to our car engine. Now imagine what it is doing to our minds. It means we never truly relax because we never venture into 2nd and 3rd gears. So, this is where meditation can play a big part in our lives. It allows us to use all four gears. It gives the brain a chance to settle down and recharge.

All forms of meditation, such as mindful awareness, self-inquiry and insight meditation are all mental practices. They are not religious, mystical or magical, just plain old practice. We are training two qualities, namely attention and meta-attention.

The first quality is easy to understand because we all know what attention means. It is focusing your awareness on something. The second quality that you train is meta-attention. Meta means a higher level, so meta-attention is a higher level of attention. This may not be so easy to understand at first.

Meta-attention is the ability to know when your focus has wandered away, which happens a lot in the early stages of learning meditation. Let's say you are focusing your awareness on your breath one moment and the next you are thinking about what you are going to have for dinner. Something knows, something tells you, "Oh, I am thinking," and that quality is meta-attention. Both of these qualities are strengthened by regular mindful awareness and meditation practices.

When practicing mindful awareness, we use the breath to anchor us to the present moment. When our minds wander off to the past or the future we simply focus our attention on the breath and return to the present moment. An easy way to do this is by practicing calming breaths. This is simply a practice of slowly and deeply breathing in through the nose and then breathing all the air out through our mouths. You can do this for as long as you wish, but at least do it three times. This really is a simple and effective practice, so try it and experience the benefits for yourself.

This simple breathing exercise not only brings us back to the present moment but also helps us change our perspective. It gives us the space to look at what is happening in a more open-minded way and helps us make clearer choices. So, the breath is an important tool to help you develop mindful awareness. With this in mind, I will guide you through a short Mindful Breathing Awareness Practice. This is the perfect way to start your journey towards a peaceful mind.

By doing this practice on a daily basis, you will gain a sense of familiarity with your breath. You will begin to understand that the breath is the bridge between your mind and your body. By slowing down your breathing, you will calm the mind and relax the body. We should always be breathing from our abdomen, so a good way to check to see if we are is by placing one hand on the chest and one on the stomach. If you are breathing from the chest it could indicate stress. So, intentionally start to breathe from the stomach. Exaggerate your breathing by pushing out your stomach on the in breath and suck it in on the out breath. Carry on doing this until you start to naturally breath from the stomach.

When you sit down to do this practice let go of any preconceived ideas of what the breath should be like. Explore, feel and listen to it. You will see that your breath is different when you are happy, sad, emotional, stressed or distracted. When you do this practice regularly you will be able to understand which types of breath are useful in different situations. For example, when you are angry, you will start to know that a good way to calm down the anger is to slow down your breathing. When you are feeling heavy and lazy, you will start to see that the best way to give yourself more energy, is to speed your breathing up.

This practice is going to be the main ingredient on your journey of self-discovery. There will be different mindful meditations in the book, but it is important to start whatever practice you are doing with this mindful awareness of the breath meditation. It will ensure your mind is settled, calm, open and ready to start whatever meditation you are going to do.

I encourage you to do this breathing awareness practice each morning before you engage with the day. This allows you to start the day with a calm, present and focused mind. You will be better able to face whatever the world throws at you.

Traditionally, in meditation, they talk about sitting in the seven-point yogic posture. I never teach this. We all have different bodies, and most of us cannot sit in this advanced posture. I believe it is more important for you to sit in a way that will allow you to be alert and relaxed at the same time. Try and sit with a straight, but not rigid, back. This will keep you alert. Then, once you have straightened your back, drop your shoulders. This will give you a relaxed posture. Remember, if you are not comfortable you will not be able to stay focused on your object of meditation. So, if sitting on the floor is difficult for you, simply sit on an unarmed chair. Your arms should be placed on your lap, so they are comfortable and will not go to sleep. I would suggest you have your eyes lightly closed. This will stop any visual distractions, but may make you sleepy, so experiment and see what works best for you. These are just guidelines, not rules. Seated in a relaxed posture you are now good to go, so let's start the breathing awareness meditation:

Sit comfortably on the floor or on an unarmed chair with your back straight, but not too rigid. Now, gently close your eyes if you wish and do the following breathing awareness exercise:

I want you to breathe in slowly and deeply through your nose to the count of 5 - pause to the count of 6 - then breathe all the air out through your mouth to the count of 7.

Again, breathe in slowly through your nose to the count of 5 - pause to the count of 6 - then breathe all the air out through your mouth to the count of 7.

One more time, breathe in slowly and deeply through your nose to the count of 5 - pause to the count of 6 - then breathe all the air out through your mouth to the count of 7.

Now breathe normally, making sure your breath is slow and natural. Don't force the breath, just let it find its own rhythm.

This exercise brings you comfortably into the present moment, the here and now.

Now I want you to bring your awareness to your breath as it flows into your nose and then back out again. There is no need to follow the breath any further. Just become aware of it entering and leaving your nose - do this for approximately 30 seconds.

If you become distracted by thoughts, noise, body pains and so on, just label the thoughts or sounds or sensations and gently bring your awareness back to your breath - do this for approximately 30 seconds.

Become aware of the sensations around your nostril and just relax into this experience - do this for approximately 30 seconds.

Just keep gently breathing, letting each breath occur naturally. Feel your breathing becoming calm...slow...easy.... continue doing this for 30 seconds.

Now, as your relaxation becomes deeper and deeper... start to count your in breaths as they flow gently. Count from 1 to 10 and then start back at 1 again - do this for approximately 90 seconds.

Now count your out breaths. Again, count from 1 to 10 and then start back at 1 again - do this for approximately 90 seconds.

Now just gently place your awareness on the breath as it enters and leaves your nose. Do not count the breaths, just be aware of them – do this for approximately one minute.

Notice how calm and relaxed you are. See how regular your breathing has become... how peaceful your breathing is - do this for as long as you wish, but for at least 90 seconds.

When you are ready, start to slowly open your eyes and look down on the floor in front of you. Stay there for at least 30 seconds to gently introduce yourself back into the world.

Don't overthink this practice, just relax into it. You are going to get many thoughts popping into your head at first, don't worry, this is totally natural. We are not trying to stop our thoughts or empty our minds – both of these are not useful. We are trying to train the mind to focus on one thing, namely, our breath. Once the mind is trained to focus solely on one thing, we can take it off the meditation cushion and out into our daily lives. Mindful awareness is all about developing awareness, being aware of what is happening right here, right now. But being totally focused like this is a skill and doing this short mindful breathing awareness practice will start to train your mind to have that skill. Just imagine the amount of pressure you can take off your mind by just concentrating on one thing at a time.

If we wish to train our mind in this way, we have to do this practice every day. Regular practice is far more important than the length of time we meditate. If we are trying to train a puppy to sit we need to do it every day. If we just did it twice a week, how would the puppy come to know what we expect from it. It's the same for our mind. If we only sit now and then the mind will never become trained. So, consistent and regular practice is of the utmost importance.

As I mentioned previously, this practice of mindful breathing is the foundation for all the other practices in this book. So, please do it several times to become familiar with it before you move on.

****

As you begin meditation practice it is useful to understand some common experiences you may encounter whilst meditating. Without this knowledge it can be quite frustrating at times.

Don't expect results straight away. Meditation isn't a quick fix. It is going to take time, as we are working with our mind, and we all know how unpredictable that can be. It will take time to learn new ways of thinking and unlearn our old outdated patterns.

Also expect a bit of physical discomfort. Just because you have seen pictures of meditators sitting cross legged on the floor, it doesn't mean that is the perfect posture for you. If it is difficult to sit cross legged on the floor, then sit on a straight-backed chair, or try a meditation bench or lay down. We are all different and we have to find a position that suits us. If you are uncomfortable you will not be relaxed, and if you are not relaxed, you will not be able to meditate.

It is common to find our mind jumping all over the place when we sit down and try to focus on one thing. It can leap from one thought to another at rapid speed. This is natural and so don't get frustrated. People who have been meditating for years have days like this. Just accept that sometimes the mind can be this way. Gently leave the thought and come back to your focus of meditation. You may have to do it over and over again but use this experience to learn patience and self-acceptance.

Boredom is another problem people can face whilst meditating. This tends to happen when we have calmed the mind but have not begun to appreciate the stillness and silence. Our minds keep themselves busy all day long and when our thoughts start to slow down, boredom creeps in. This is the point where many give up. We need to just keep going and understand that the mind doesn't need to be thinking all the time. Learn to enjoy the peace and tranquillity of a quiet mind.

The final point I want to make here is, don't fall into the trap of always looking for benefits. Of course, you want your meditation practice to do something for you, otherwise what's the point? But constantly looking for progress is going to impede your progress. Try to practice being present without wanting anything. The more you search for progress, the more you will get frustrated with meditation. Benefits will naturally come once you learn simply to let go.

Eight – Expanding Awareness

With a foundation of mindful awareness and the introduction of a breathing awareness practice to anchor us in the present moment, we are now ready to look at some more ways we can expand our awareness with mindfulness. Of course, there are many possible applications, but I will concentrate on four main foundation practices. These are mindfulness of our bodies, of our feelings, of our minds and of our mental states.

The purpose of these practices is to get to know ourselves better. It will help us understand what is working for us and what isn't. This will allow us to change more effectively and positively.

Awareness of body

The first practice is for the body. We need to be aware of our body and all the actions carried out by it. But, we do not need to see it as 'my' body. If we think of it as 'my' body, it could lead to attachment and give us a false sense of identity. Reflect on the time and effort we spend on this body just to look good. Imagine how much money is spent each year on plastic surgery and beauty products. It would appear we are completely obsessed with our bodies. We might be mindful of how the body looks but very rarely spend time on observing the actions it carries out.

There are many ways of contemplating the body, but a simple and effective one is doing a full body scan.

Sit comfortably with your back straight, but not too rigid, and drop your shoulders. Gently close your eyes and start to focus on your breath. Don't force the breath, just let it find its own rhythm. Become aware of it flowing into and out of your nose. Do this until you are relaxed and focused. Now, gently move your awareness down to your toes. Are they relaxed or tense? If they are tense, exhale and breathe the tension out. Can you feel any sensations in the toes? If so, don't judge or try to change the sensation, just observe it. If you can't feel any sensations, no problem, just move on. Do not stay on any area for more 10 seconds, as you may start to fixate on the area or the sensation. This exercise is teaching you how to reconnect to the body, but more importantly, it is teaching you how to observe without getting all tangled up with the sensations. This will help you when you come to look at the other applications of mindfulness.

Now, to continue with the practice, move to your feet and do the same. Slowly move up your body, watching where the tension is, releasing it and then focusing on any sensations that may be present. When you have scanned the whole of your body, take your awareness back to the breath and spend a few moments focusing on the breath flowing in and out of your nose. When you are ready you can slowly begin to open your eyes.

In today's world, we always seem to be running from pillar to post, so this meditation will help you get back in tune with the body and calm your mind at the same time. I am sure you will be surprised at how much tension you are carrying around with you and what different sensations you have in various parts of the body.

The full body scan is one of my favourite practices and I am always surprised at the sensations I am carrying around. Over the years I have noticed certain sensations correspond to different emotions and experiences. When I was young I started to have asthma and I noticed that 10 to 15 minutes before an attack I would start to get an itching sensation under my chin. This gave me ample time to take my tablet and prevent the attack from taking hold. Many sensations in the body are there for a reason, but unfortunately, we have lost the art of reading our bodies and rely too much on our minds. This application of mindful awareness will bring you back in touch with your body.

As we become more in touch with our bodies you may ask how can we can integrate this awareness in our daily practice? Whatever you do with the body affects you and those around you. So, this is where a daily reflective practice will help you. Look back on the day and see what actions you have carried out with the body. The ones that are conducive to responsible living should be noted. This will ensure that, through repetition, they can become spontaneous. The ones that are not conducive to living responsibly should also be noted and a clear effort should be made to refrain from doing them again. It is through staying mindful of our bodily actions that we will be able to live responsibly.

Awareness of feelings

Another application for mindful awareness is feelings. Now, I am not talking about emotions here, many people get the two mixed up. Emotions are mental states whereas feelings arise when our senses come into contact with something. There are three types of feelings, namely pleasant, unpleasant and neutral. One of these three are present during every moment of our experience. They may be strong or weak, but they are always present.

Here are some examples of how feelings occur. You may be walking down the street and you pass a good-looking person, this brings up pleasant feelings. As you walk further, a dog barks at you and unpleasant feelings arise. A bit later, you walk past a group of people you do not know, none of them are of interest to you, so you have a neutral feeling.

If we are not mindful and leave our feelings unchecked, pleasant feelings can lead to clinging desires, painful feelings to hatred and neutral feelings to apathy. When paying attention to feelings, the important thing is simply to notice them, become aware of them, without either clinging to them or pushing them away.

Here are two ways we can mindfully get in touch with our feelings. Firstly, during meditation, after you have spent some time watching your breath, notice what comes into your mind and observe what feeling is attached to that experience. Don't try to change or judge the feeling, just become aware of it and then let it go on its way. Then do the same with the next object that comes into your mind. You can do this for as long as you like and then return back to your breathing awareness. This practice helps you notice how you feel and what's going on with you. It also helps you to understand that a feeling is present in every experience you have.

As with your awareness of your body you can also review your feelings during your daily reflective practice. When you think of an incident that happened that day, check to see what feelings it invoked in you. Did it bring up pleasant, painful or neutral feelings? Don't try to control the feelings, just be mindful of them.

Being watchful of our feelings helps us see what desires we are chasing when a pleasant feeling is present and what is being invoked by our unpleasant feelings. We can also learn to simply observe an experience, without getting all tangled up in it. This will help us to form neutral responses, instead of getting attached to pleasant feelings or repelled by unpleasant feelings.

Awareness of mind

The next area of focus is on our minds. We can apply mindful awareness to explore deep into our minds. If I am honest, this was always the most difficult for me to get my head around. How can the mind look at itself? The answer that came to me is that we look at the mind as though we are looking in a mirror. When we talk about the mind we tend to think of it as a single thing, but it is actually a sequence of instances that arise from moment to moment in response to the perceptions coming to us from the six senses - things we see, hear, smell, taste, and touch and from internal mental states. The mind is a process and cannot exist alone. So, when we look at the mind we are actually looking at the processing going on in the brain.

We rarely stop and spend time observing our minds. We just let thoughts, hopes, fears and dreams come and go unchecked. But our minds, if left unrestrained, can lead us into all kinds of situations. So, we practice simply observing our minds. We do not engage with what we see – we just allow it to arise and go. I understand that this is easier said than done, but with practice, patience and effort, it is achievable.

During your meditation or a daily reflective practice, observe your mind and see what state it is in: is it tired, lazy, angry, happy or disturbed? Note the state, but don't try to change it. Ask yourself, "How is my mind at the moment?" "Is it full of desire, full of anger, or full of ignorance. Is it present in the moment or distracted?" We need to look at our mind in this way, and just see it as it is, not pass any judgement or think of it as 'my mind'.

You can also focus your awareness on the way each thought arises, remains and then moves away. This helps us to stop blindly following one thought after another. We gain insight and understand that we are not our thoughts and we do not need to chase after each and every one. In fact, we cannot find any part of our mind to identify with, it is just a constantly changing process.

Once you have learned how to dispassionately watch your mind, whenever your mind is disturbed, you should firstly examine it and then, with calmness, act in a proper way – a way that is not going to harm yourself or others. Developing awareness of the mind will help us lead a life where we are not becoming disturbed or disturbing others. We come to know the mind as it really is – a process.

Awareness of mental states

The final application of mindfulness is concerning mental states. A mental state is an awareness of objects that come in contact with our senses, which occur on a moment to moment basis. As we bring awareness to these moments of consciousness, we begin to strengthen our ability to take mindfulness into our daily lives.

There are positive mental states, such as happiness, compassion, empathy, contentment, and negative mental states, such as greed, apathy, anger, selfishness and so on.

We are not looking to oppose these mental states, but just become aware of them, acknowledge them and, if they are negative mental states, let them go. There are several ways of letting the mental states go and here are the ones that have worked for me.

You can change the negative into a positive, such as replacing greed with generosity or hatefulness with compassion. Thinking of the consequences of the negative mindset can be another way of letting go. If we understand that this mindset is leading us down a wrong path, we should not follow it. We could for example bring to mind the insight that all things that arise are impermanent, the negative mental factor is not going to last, so just let it go. Finally, and probably the most difficult, is to detach totally from the mental state. Let's face it, we manage to detach totally from reality sometimes, even when it is staring us in the face. With practice we are able to detach from our mental states. All of these practices are not easy, but they are doable, it just takes effort.

We should also look to meditate on mental factors and here is a suggested practice.

As I mentioned before, sit comfortably with your back straight, but not too rigid, and drop your shoulders. Start by focusing on your breath. Don't force the breath, just let it find its own rhythm. Become aware of it flowing into and out of your nose. Feel yourself becoming relaxed and focused.

When a mental state arises, and it will, if it is strong enough to disrupt your focus on the breath, rest your awareness in that new state, allowing yourself to be aware of what the state is, such as joyful mind or angry mind, fearful mind or contented mind, until it naturally subsides. If the mental state is strong, notice what it feels like in the body. Is there tightness, discomfort, pain? Where is it located?

Now look at the consequences of this mental state. Will it lead to a sense of peace in your life or lead to more difficulty? Remember, you should not judge these states of mind, simply bring awareness to them.

If another mental state arises and is strong enough to hold your attention, continue to practice with it. If one doesn't, then return to watching your breath until your meditation session has finished.

This brings us to the end of mindful awareness applications. If we are going to be mindful, and live a responsible life we have to be fully aware of, but not tangled up in, our bodies, our feelings, our minds and our mental states. By being mindful, we will be able to take full responsibility for all of our actions. This will ensure that our minds become calmer and we spend more time in the present moment, not being tossed backwards and forwards from past to future. Being mindful means being conscious of every thought, feeling, emotion and action. Repeatedly during the day, take a few moments to bring mindful awareness to your breath, body sensations, mind, feelings and mental states. This is a good way of helping yourself to settle down into the present moment and to expand your formal meditation practices into your everyday life.

Nine - Strength of Mind

Now I want us to look at another key element of the mind that we need to work on, namely, single-pointed awareness.

We become distracted very easily and find it hard to stay focused for any length of time. The mind lurches from one thing to another at a rapid speed, and then we wonder why our mind is not at peace. How can it be, it's exhausted! So, learning how to stay focused on a single object, thought, emotion, feeling, body sensation or experience is going to cut down on distractions and help strengthen our minds.

Years ago, when I used to get home from working in Central London, my mind was totally drained. Physically I was fine, but mentally, I had a job to string a useful sentence together. It wasn't that my job was over taxing, it was more to do with me overloading my brain. It was at that time I started to really understand the benefits of mindfulness and meditation. I started to realise that peace and tranquillity come about through single-pointed awareness. I began to focus on the job at hand and not let my senses overload my mind.

One of the best ways to achieve single-pointed awareness is through meditation. The mindful meditations I have mentioned earlier all need a foundation of single-pointed awareness to be effective. In those meditations we focused on the breath, body, feelings, mind and mental states.

To achieve the most from meditation you also need to like, or have a positive attitude, about the practice. It's a long-term process. It isn't enough to do a 10-day meditation course and think job done. That is just the starting point. If we want to live peaceful, purposeful and fruitful lives we need to develop a mind of resilience and mettle. Without fortitude of mind we will never achieve peace.

To have strength of mind, four mental qualities need to be developed. These are purpose, persistence, sensitivity and analysis.

What's your purpose?

When I first started meditating many thoughts would pop into my head and start to hamper my meditation practice. I would suddenly start busying myself with non-essential work just to delay meditating. It was easy to lose interest because I wasn't seeing any immediate results. I even started to lack confidence because I thought I wasn't doing it right. This was all happening because I hadn't set clear goals or purpose for my practice. I just sat down and started meditating because I heard it was good for me.

So, the starting point to strengthening your mind is to understand why you are doing the practice, what you would like to achieve and how you will know when you have achieved it. All of these will give you a sense of purpose.

If you wish to succeed in meditation it is important to like the process. We need to allow it to capture our imagination and then it will become easier to get absorbed in it. We cannot just go through the motions and hope it magically leads us to where we want to be. We must have a purpose, an objective.

When we go to the gym our objective is to become fitter. When we go on a diet the purpose is to lose weight. When we learn a musical instrument, we do so because we wish to play it proficiently. My point here is that whenever we start something we should always have an anticipated outcome that guides our planned actions.

If we don't have a purpose in meditation we are very soon going to lose interest because we will have no vision of where we want to go and what we want to achieve.

Meditation is a practice and as with all other practices, we need to be aware of how much attention we are paying to it, how closely we observe what we are doing, how effective we are being and how much our personal wellbeing is improving. By looking at these points your practice is going to improve.

So, take some time to reflect on these questions:

What are your reasons for practicing mindfulness and meditation?

How are you going to measure your progress?

How will you know when you have achieved your purpose?

Do you think you can achieve it or is it a never-ending journey?

Once you have made all these points clear in your mind, you will have your purpose and will be ready to move onto the next point.

Can you persist?

Even though we may have a clear purpose to practice, without persistence, success will evade you. To simply have a purpose is not enough, we need to take action. Otherwise, our purpose becomes ineffective and intellectual.

Single-pointed awareness can only be gained through a force of effort and persistence. When these are applied diligently and in a balanced way, only then can our awareness become single-pointed. When I say balance, I mean not too forceful and not too lax. Consider how a guitar string needs to be tuned for it to give a perfect note. If it is too loose or too tight you will not strike the right sound. Our persistence in the same way needs to be tuned.

If you get too wrapped up or enthusiastic with your practice and cannot stop doing it, you are likely to burn out. If you only do it on rare occasions, you will never be able to train the mind. Balance is required to tune your practice.

We have to be willing to put in effort, even though the results may not be noticed immediately. It is no good just to do a meditation practice when we feel like it. I understand that it is not easy to sit when we are tired, or to sit through pain or even sit for extra minutes, but if we don't, we are not going to progress on the path.

If we only sit when we feel like it, that is all we are going to know: the mind that likes to sit. We will never get to explore the mind that doesn't like to sit. So, we need the attitude of, "Oh! The meditation is not going well, I need to discover why." The more you look at the mind that doesn't like to sit, the more you understand it and find ways to work with it. If you give in at the first hurdle you will never fully understand your mind.

It is inevitable that there are going to be times when you can't be bothered to do the practice, or you are too busy or too tired. These are the times we really need to stick with it and push through any obstacles we may have created in our mind. This is a key point to remember, these obstacles are all created by your mind. You are the one stopping yourself from meditating.

Before you move on, take a moment to think about how much effort and persistence you will need to bring about changes in your life. What would be a good balance between too much and too little practice? Set yourself redlines, as this will help keep you on track. Remember, meditation isn't a punishment, so if you step over your redline at some point, don't get angry or frustrated, just resolve to try harder to stay within your boundaries next time.

Are you sensitive?

The next strength is sensitivity. We need to be sensitive about what we are trying to gain from the meditation, what effort we are putting in and what progress we are making.

We also need to be sensitive to what state our mind is in when we come to meditation. Sometimes our mind is overactive and at other times underactive. When this happens, you need to strengthen the mind before you focus on your object of meditation. If you are overactive, you can slow your breathing down. You can also ensure you are breathing from your abdominal region and not your chest. When you are underactive, you can speed your breath up a little. You could even do some light stretching exercises to wake yourself up, such as yoga, mindful movement or Tai Chi.

Try to be fully aware and engaged with what you are doing and what results you are getting. Understand that you are not looking for future achievements or looking back over past experiences, you are being sensitive to what is happening right now, right in this moment.

When we are breathing, we need to be sensitive to each breath. When we are sitting, we need to be sensitive to how it feels to sit. When we look at our minds as though we are looking in a mirror, we need to be sensitive to our mental state. We have to be watchful of every aspect of the meditation.

Going through the motions is just not going to cut it. You have to make the practice your practice, and we do that by having a purpose, putting in effort and being sensitive to what is happening during the meditation.

So, how sensitive are you to your practice? Look at these following points. Are you sensitive to the effort you are putting in? Sensitive to your state of mind before, during and after meditation? Sensitive to the quality of your breath or any other object of meditation? Sensitive to what hindrances are stopping you from meditating?

Do you analyse?

Analysing is another key to strengthen the mind. We need to clearly examine our tendency to fall into bad habits and wrong practices. It also involves learning to work with an imperfect mind and balancing our mental faculties.

We need to analyse our meditation practice and not just sit there and hope for the best. If the mind is in no mood to focus on your object of meditation, don't give up, investigate other topics your mind may wish to focus on. Try something different, like focusing on a candle flame, chanting or focus on body sensations. Explore new possibilities. If your new approach works, continue with it. If you notice it is not really working, be willing to stop doing it and try a fresh approach.

I learned this the hard way. I was given a practice and I ploughed on for over a year, even though it simply wasn't working. I foolishly believed that my teacher knew better. We need to understand that we are all different and there isn't one practice that suits everyone. We must analyse our practices until we find one that works for us. Now, I am not encouraging you to flit from one practice to another. Once you find a practice that works, stick with it, but until you find one that works it is fine to experiment with different meditation styles. Remember, we are not looking for the most popular practice or a practice that proclaims it will lead you to enlightenment. We are looking for a practice that works for us. A practice that will calm our minds and make our lives less crazy.

If you already have a practice, think about it for a moment.

What do you do when your chosen focus of meditation isn't working?

Do you walk away, persevere or are you willing to try a new approach?

These are questions for you to ponder.

That brings us to the end of how we can strengthen our minds through various meditation practices. I hope you have understood that more than anything else, it's what you bring to the meditation that determines the results you'll get. This places the responsibility and the power with you.

Ten - Essentials of Meditation

This is the final piece of the jigsaw I have called practices. All these pieces put together as a whole will help you understand the importance of meditation to navigate the choppy waters of your mind. In the last few chapters you have received a thorough introduction into the practice of mindfulness meditation. With that as a solid foundation it is now time to move onto self-inquiry meditation – also known as insight or analytical meditation. But before that, let's look at the essentials of a beneficial meditation practice.

I deliberately used the word beneficial because we shouldn't really be characterising our meditation practice as good or bad, even though such comparisons come easy to us. What I am talking about, when I say a beneficial practice, are that certain qualities will make your practice more productive, easier and enjoyable for you to sit down and meditate.

You bring me joy

Meditation often begins when we realise that we have spent so much of our lives trying to chase or buy happiness, and let's be honest, it hasn't really worked, has it? We see clearly that there is no true and lasting happiness to be found in accumulating possessions. They may make us happy for a short time, but it never lasts. The item we bought breaks, stops working, gets stolen or just becomes outdated. That's the nature of possessions, they are impermanent. We become frustrated with the normal search for happiness and start looking for something different and more meaningful. So, we turn to meditation.

Once we understand this crucial point, that we will never truly be happy with external objects, we start to let go of our craving desires, and allow for the possibility of the joy of living in the present moment. This brings a more lasting joy and understanding this is the first essential point. We begin to see that real joy arises from what we do and not what we own. This joy is an inner phenomenon and cannot be bought. Understanding this brings a feeling of contentment and gratefulness, and this leads to real joy. We spend more time meditating and less time craving. When we are excited about meditating, and not forcing ourselves to sit down on the meditation cushion, we are using the factor of joy.

This sense of joy with meditation takes time and effort, but it is totally achievable, and once you begin to feel the benefits, joy will arise. You will not need to force yourself to sit, you will totally want to. I can assure you; this is such a liberating feeling.

Oh! peace and quiet at last

Tranquillity is the second essential point, and this refers to our ability to relax. This is important for any meditator because if we make ourselves stressed about the meditation or try too hard, it may end up turning us away from our practice, or at the very least, make us uncomfortable with it. So, tranquillity reflects our ability to manage stress and tension. A turbulent mind filled with uncontrolled thoughts drains our energy, leaving us completely tired, exhausted and frustrated. When I first started meditating I was concentrating so much it left me with a headache. I had less tranquillity after meditation than I did before I started. No one explained to me that meditation can be filled with joy and tranquillity. In those days meditation was a chore and joy and tranquillity weren't even in the picture. Thankfully, someone taught me these essentials of meditation and my whole practice turned around.

The tranquillity I am talking about is relaxation of both body and mind. When we are new to meditation we tend to try too hard and worry if we are doing it correctly. Both things cause us to be uncomfortable and lack single-pointed focus. So, we need to approach our practice with a calm mind and a relaxed body. I would suggest you do some simple stretching exercises before you sit down, so your body is nice and relaxed. Once you have sat down, focus your awareness on your breath and take some slow, deep breaths to calm your mind.

Remember, we can't force a state of tranquillity. It arises naturally from being relaxed, calm and joyful.

Keep your mind on the job

Focus is the next essential point. We need to focus all of our mental faculties on one physical or mental object, such as our breath, body sensations, an image or a lit candle.

We slow down our mental activity through single-pointed focus. In this state, subject and object are completely absorbed into one. We have the tendency to split things into self and other, like and dislike, love and hate and so on. When we are meditating single-pointedly this dualistic thinking disappears.

Focusing is our ability to keep awareness on a single object, without distraction. When we count our breaths during meditation, that is focus. When we stay unblinkingly aware of a candle flame or a statue that is focus. When we visualise something in our minds, that is focus. We are trying to keep our mind on a single object and stop it wandering off.

It is only the tranquil mind that can easily focus on a subject of meditation. So, it is important to strengthen your joy and tranquillity first.

Once we have achieved joy, tranquillity and focus we are then able to start analysing. This is the next form of meditation. Developing focus is called stabilising meditation.

Let me briefly discuss the difference between these meditation practices.

Stabilising meditation seeks to focus one's attention on a chosen object, such as the breath, a mantra or a statue. The mindful awareness of the breath meditation, previously mentioned, is also a form of stabilising meditation.

We always start our meditation practice with a stabilising practice and then move on to other types of meditation. This is so our minds are relaxed, calm and able to focus.

I see you

Self-inquiry meditation is an intense investigation into the nature of reality and into the nature of our own mind. This deep analysis can bring insights that help strengthen positive states of mind and overcome those negative attitudes, thoughts and emotions that lead to emotional suffering.

When I introduced a Reflective Practice in a previous chapter I stated that there are three aspects to self-awareness, namely emotional awareness, self-evaluation and self-confidence. In self-inquiry meditation, emotional awareness refers to what you are feeling right now, what your emotional experience is in this present moment. Self-evaluation investigates questions such as 'Is this who I am?' 'Is this who I want to be?' 'Is this what I like, and is this what I don't like?' Emotional awareness and self-evaluation developed in these ways leads to self-confidence because as we learn about ourselves, once we truly know ourselves, we become more confident and self-assured.

Self-inquiry meditation opens our awareness to all aspects of our environment, our habitual thinking and our sense of self. It opens our mind to those thoughts, feelings or impulses that you might normally try to suppress.

Sometimes, even though we may recognise that some of our beliefs are wrong, they are often so deep rooted that they may seem virtually impossible to get rid of. By doing self-inquiry meditation, we can deconstruct these beliefs, examining the concepts we cling to and question whether they are helpful or not. Practicing this way, logic becomes more sustainable, leading to peace of mind.

During our analytical meditation sessions, we can examine both our inner and outer worlds. So, let's look at an example of what it means to scrutinise these worlds.

All of our outer possessions are impermanent. All things are compounded, meaning they are made up of two or more things. Things come together for a period of time and then break up, disintegrate, die or change in some other way. Let's take a car for instance, we label it car as though it is one solid, permanent thing, but of course it isn't because it is made up of many different parts. These different parts are all impermanent and so are constantly changing. Your tyres wear out, the paintwork gets scratched or fades, the lights blow, the windshield shatters and so on. What we see as a permanent car is actually many different parts in constant flux.

By analysing things in this way during our meditation session, we begin to understand that all things are subject to change. We will firstly comprehend this logically, then on a deeper level.

The point of this exercise is to stop ourselves getting attached to all forms of outer phenomena, because whenever we become attached to something, we invariably cause ourselves emotional suffering.

We do not just see outside objects as permanent, we believe we are permanent too.

I am sure intellectually we know we are not permanent, but we chose not to face up to it. This causes us to get attached to our bodies, thoughts, feelings and emotions, which in turn causes us emotional suffering. If we meditate on our bodies, we will see that they are changing moment by moment. The same goes for our thoughts, feelings, emotions, experiences and perceptions. We are not the solid, permanent entities we believe we are. We are changing every moment. Below is a meditation practice on impermanence that will guide you through this process.

Obviously, there is no end to what you can analyse during your meditation practice, from bad habits, being ego driven, anger, lack of empathy and so on, but the three most important ones for gaining peace of mind are compassion, impermanence and death. Below are three self-inquiry meditations to develop understanding in these areas. The first two are more suited for beginners, whist the third one is more advanced as it asks you to face death in a more direct way. All three of these guided meditations can be found on the Buddhism Guide app.

Compassion Awareness Meditation:

Sit comfortably and lightly close your eyes. We'll start by doing three calming breaths.

Breathe in slowly and deeply through your nose...hold the breath...breathe the air out through your mouth.

Again, breathe in through your nose...hold the breath...breathe the air out through your mouth.

One more time, breathe in...hold...breathe out.

Now breath normally and don't force the breath, just let it find its own rhythm.

I believe the definition of compassion is, 'the wish to free others from suffering.'

Think about these words for a moment. (pause for 30 seconds)

Is this how you would describe compassion? (pause for 30 seconds)

I want you to look at compassion through your own experience.

What does it feel like to have compassion towards others? (pause for one minute)

What does it feel like when others show compassion towards you? (pause for one minute)

Now think about what it feels like when you lose your compassion for others? You stop caring about them and your heart closes down. (pause for one minute)

What does it feel like when others lose compassion for you. (pause for one minute)

Think of a time when you were going through a difficult period in your life and no one cared – what did it feel like? (pause for one minute)

Now, think of a time when you showed compassion towards someone. (pause)

What emotions do you feel? (pause for 30 seconds)

What body sensations do you feel? (pause for 30 seconds)

What benefits did you gain from giving compassion? (pause for 30 seconds)

Now, think of a time when you were shown compassion by someone. (pause)

What emotions do you feel? (pause for 30 seconds)

What body sensations do you feel? (pause for 30 seconds)

What benefits did you gain from receiving compassion? (pause for 30 seconds)

Now, just sit for a moment with the warmth of compassion in your heart. (pause for 30 seconds)

Now, very slowly open your eyes and sit there a moment to allow yourself to return to the outside world.

Impermanence Awareness Meditation:

Sit comfortably and lightly close your eyes. Let's start by doing three calming breaths.

Breathe in slowly and deeply through your nose...hold the breath...breathe the air out through your mouth.

Again, breathe in through your nose...hold the breath...breathe the air out through your mouth.

One more time, breathe in...hold...breathe out.

Now breath normally and don't force the breath, just let it find its own rhythm.

Everything is subject to death and decay; our possessions, friends, family and even our physical bodies. Life is like an unstoppable river rushing towards the ocean.

I want you to look back over your life, at all the things you have seen, the things you have done, the places you have been. (pause for 30 seconds)

Now look back at all the people you've met in your life. Where are they now? (pause for 30 seconds)

Now think back to when you were younger. See how the years have changed you emotionally, mentally and physically. (pause for 30 seconds)

We are now going to contemplate the five remembrances.

Firstly, contemplate this - I am sure to grow old, I cannot avoid aging. (pause for 30 seconds)

Now, contemplate this - I am sure to get sick, I cannot avoid illness. (pause for 30 seconds)

Now contemplate - I am sure to die, I cannot avoid death. (pause for 30 seconds)

Contemplate the fourth remembrance - I must be parted from all that is dear and beloved to me. (pause for 30 seconds)

Finally, contemplate this - I am the owner and the heir of my actions. I will reap the fruit of my actions, for better or worse. (pause for 30 seconds)

Before we finish, I want you to see if these remembrances have helped loosen your attachment to people, possessions or your physical body. (pause for 30 seconds)

Now, very slowly open your eyes and sit there a moment to allow yourself to return to the outside world.

Death Awareness Meditation:

Before we start the meditation, I want to say a few words. Death is an emotive subject and maybe not something you like to think about. But it's important for us to face our fears and not run away from them. If you want to know about life, first deal with death. If, whilst doing this meditation, you become overwhelmed, then just stop and gently open your eyes. You can always return to it another day. If you are already feeling emotional, anxious, depressed or fearful, then I would strongly suggest you do not start the meditation. It may make matters worse.

Now, sit comfortably and lightly close your eyes. Let's start by doing three calming breaths.

Breathe in slowly and deeply through your nose...hold the breath...breathe the air out through your mouth.

Again, breathe in through your nose...hold the breath...breathe the air out through your mouth.

One more time, breathe in...hold...breathe out.

Now breath normally and don't force the breath, just let it find its own rhythm.

Although death is the only thing that's certain in life, we don't usually plan for it. But it's important to think about and be prepared for it. So, contemplate the following points to get a sense of death awareness.

Everyone has to die. So, to generate an experience of the inevitability of death, bring to mind famous people from the past who you know have died. (pause for 30 seconds)

Now bring to mind people you personally know who have already died. (pause for 30 seconds)

And now think of the people you know who are still alive. Contemplate that each of these people will one day die and so will you. Try to experience this fact using your feelings, thoughts and emotions. (pause for 30 seconds)

Now contemplate that your lifespan is decreasing continuously. Seconds become minutes, minutes become hours, hours become days, days become years, and as time is passing in this way, you are travelling closer and closer towards death. Your life is like a fast-flowing river, experience this uninterrupted flow of time carrying you to the end of your life. Hold your awareness on this for a while, and check what thoughts and feelings arise in your mind. (pause for 30 seconds)

The amount of time you have for developing your mind is very small. Since you are getting closer and closer to death day by day, how much time do you spend consciously trying to improve your state of mind, or doing beneficial things such as helping others, or spiritual study or meditation? What are you doing to prepare for your death? (pause for 30 seconds)

How much time do you spend working on decreasing the negative aspects of the mind and developing the positive aspects, and behaving in ways that are beneficial to others? (pause for 10 seconds)

Be honest, is it enough time? (pause for 30 seconds)

By meditating on these points, you should be able to develop the determination to use your life wisely and mindfully.

The next contemplation is on how human life-expectancy is uncertain. Life can end at any point: at birth, in childhood, in adolescence or middle age – we really can't tell. Think of examples of people you know or have heard about who died before they reached the age you are now. (pause for 30 seconds)

Being young and healthy is no guarantee that a person will live a long time— children sometimes die before their parents. Healthy people can die before those who are suffering. You might think that death is not going to happen for a long time. Why do you think this way? Is there any way you can know for sure when death will happen? (pause for 30 seconds)

Generate a strong feeling of the uncertainty of your own time of death; how there is simply no guarantee that you have long to live. (30 seconds)

There are many different ways that death can happen. Death can happen due to external causes, such as natural disasters, or accidents, or you could be killed by another person or by dangerous animals. Contemplate how many ways you can die from external causes. (pause for 30 seconds)

Death can also happen due to internal causes, such as diseases. Contemplate how many different diseases you can die of. (pause for 30 seconds)

Bring to mind cases of people you know or have heard about who have died and think of how they died. Think that any of these things could happen to you as well. (pause for 30 seconds)

Our human body is very vulnerable; it can be injured or struck down by illness so easily. Within minutes it can change from being strong and active to being helplessly weak and full of pain. The difference between life and death is one breath.

Right now, you might feel healthy, energetic and secure, but something as small as a virus or as insignificant as a paper cut could become the cause of your death. Recall the times you have hurt or injured your body, and how easily it could happen again and even cause your death. (pause for 30 seconds)

Your body will not last forever. Soon it will degenerate, lose its beauty and vitality and finally die. Think about how much your body has changed over the years. (pause for 30 seconds)

No matter how many friends and family we have, no matter how much wealth, power, possessions we have, none of it goes with us at death. Think about that for a moment. (pause for 30 seconds)

We should aim to die at peace with ourselves, feeling good about how we lived our life, and not leaving behind any unresolved conflicts with people. The only thing that will truly benefit us at the time of death are positive states of mind such as compassion, patience and wisdom. But to be able to have such states of mind at the time of death, we need to make ourselves familiar with them during the course of our lives. Are you ready for death? What do you need to do to make yourself ready? (pause for 30 seconds)

What attachments will you have at the time of death? Our strongest attachments are usually to our family and friends, so you would probably think of them, and feel a strong desire to be with them. But your loved ones cannot help you when you are on your deathbed. They may love you very much, but they cannot stop you from dying. When we die, we go alone. Recognise the attachment you have to your family and friends. Think about how your attachment will prevent you from dying peacefully. (pause for 30 seconds)

At the time of death, your mind will probably also think of your possessions. But can any of these things bring you comfort and peace at the time of death? Your wealth may be able to provide you with the best medical care, but that is all it can do for you. It cannot stop death from happening, and when you die, you cannot take any of it with you. Contemplate these points and see if you can understand the importance of learning to be less dependent on and attached to material things. (pause for 30 seconds)

Your body has been your constant companion since birth. You have cared for it and protected it, worried about it, kept it healthy, fed it and cleaned it, experienced all kinds of pleasure and pain with it. But now you are dying you will be separated from it. It will become weak and useless. Soon it will be taken to the cemetery or crematorium. What good can it possibly do you now? Contemplate the strong sense of attachment you have towards your body. Can it benefit you in any way at death? (pause for 30 seconds)

You may feel fearful and sad whilst doing this meditation. That's not the point of the meditation, but a bit of fear and sadness can be a motivator. It is important to get in touch with how you feel about death, so that you can work on being prepared for it when it happens. We should not want to die with a negative state of mind or regrets about how we have lived our lives. You need to get a strong sense of how terrible it would be to die like that, so that you live your life wisely, doing as many positive, beneficial things as possible. (pause for 30 seconds)

Now, very slowly open your eyes and sit there a moment to allow yourself to return to the outside world.

****

Steady as she goes

Equanimity is the final essential quality. It is that ability to walk a middle path between the extremes of aversion and desire. In other words, it is not letting your mind be pulled this way and that by what you like and dislike.

It is sometimes referred to as an evenness of mind or a non-dual mind.

During meditation, equanimity helps us see phenomena arise and then pass away with a calm and tranquil mind. We don't see good and bad, like and dislike; we only see non-dual awareness. A thought may arise, you may be distracted by a sound or body sensation, whatever distraction arises, you simply watch it arise and go. This is equanimity.

Some people get confused about what equanimity means. It is not indifference or a lack of care. In fact, it is opposite to that and the less we judge, criticise and conceptualise the more compassionate and empathic we are.

****

Before you move onto the next part of the book, here are the main points that have been covered so far.

- Most of our emotional suffering is caused by ourselves because of the way we live our lives, because of our beliefs, biases, concepts and social conditioning.

- What we are searching for in life is to reduce our suffering, physical and emotional, and have a peaceful mind.
- There are three types of suffering; suffering of pain, the suffering of change and all-pervasive suffering.
- There are many causes of suffering, but the three main ones are aversion, attachment and clinging desire.
- It is important to set ourselves redlines as these will keep our actions in check and allow us to start reducing the avoidable emotional suffering in our lives.
- It is extremely beneficial to introduce a daily reflection practice into your daily routine. This entails looking back over the day and reinforcing what worked for you and then looking at what didn't work so well. This practice allows you to examine why it didn't work and how you could act in a more beneficial way next time.
- You are going to encounter many obstacles or hindrances on this journey

of self-discovery. Some common ones are sensual desires, ill-will, lack of enthusiasm, anxiety and doubt.

- We cannot be mindfully aware all of the time because we have the ability to plan for the future and look back over the past. So, it is important to learn various mindful awareness practice, such as STOP, breathing awareness, body scan and so on, as these will bring you back in touch with whatever is happening in the here and now. In this present moment we are able to mindfully respond and not just blindly react.

- Further mindful awareness practices are awareness of the body, awareness of feelings, awareness of the mind and awareness of mental states.

- It is important to strengthen our minds through single-pointed awareness, as this will prevent us from becoming easily distracted and allow us to strengthen our focus. To have strength of mind, four mental qualities need to be developed. These are purpose, persistence, sensitivity and analysis.

- Meditation is like any other practice, you need to establish certain qualities. In this case, for a fruitful meditation, you require joy, tranquillity, focus and analysis.

If you have forgotten or are unsure about any of these points, I suggest you go back and reread that chapter. This is a reference book and as such should become your meditation and mindfulness companion. So, to get the most out of the book don't read it once and then place it on your bookshelf. Leave it close at hand, so you can refer to it whenever you have doubts or need guidance or encouragement.

Part Three
Path

Eleven – Controlling Factors

Before I take you through the eight stages of the path, I want to introduce you to five valuable qualities, which are going to be helpful while journeying along this path. Although you may possess these qualities to some degree they need to be developed and cultivated until they become dominant and controlling factors.

These qualities are useful in developing any skill, be it training in a sport, playing a musical instrument or meditation. The qualities are confidence, vigour, vigilance, focus and discernment.

Confidence

Before we can start any project, path or new venture, we first have to have confidence. This confidence is not a blind faith, but confidence based on reasoning and investigation. Without it we probably wouldn't even start on a new path. It helps encourage us as we apply ourselves and begin to experience results. The more confident we become, the more fully we will engage with the path. It has been described as the seed that gives rise to a fruit bearing tree. Meaning, your confidence will grow and eventually come to fruition.

At the beginning, our confidence may be inspired by someone or something we read or heard. After some time, we start to learn from our own experiences. Our confidence grows as it is verified. For example, you heard that mindful meditation is good for reducing stress, you have never tried it but as so many people are talking about it you have the confidence to give it a try. After a while, you begin to see some results, you are now practicing because of your own experience.

I always found it hard to believe that there was some external superpower that had control over my life. This is what drew me to meditation. I had heard that if you meditate you will be able to tame your mind and gain the ability to change the things in your life that are not working for you. This gave me the confidence to join a meditation group. I had no idea if it would work or not, but because I had read a lot about it, I thought I would give it a go. Now I know from my own experience that meditation really does work. I am so pleased that I had the confidence to take the first steps. My life has changed immensely because of it.

So, the first valuable quality one needs on the path is strong confidence, as strong as a cable that holds a ship to its anchor in stormy weather.

Vigour

Once we have confidence, we need to then put in the effort to be able to move along the path. This is where the valuable quality of vigour comes into play.

Learning new tasks takes vigour, doing a regular meditation practice takes vigour, becoming fluent in a foreign language takes vigour and so does keeping ourselves on the right path.

There may be days where our will-power is low, or our emotions are high, and we are simply finding it hard to stay on track. It is at these times we need to redouble our efforts.

It is not just about having the required effort to start a particular path, we also have to have the effort to sustain it despite obstacles, and then have the effort to continue throughout our lives. Staying on the path is a lifetime work and we shouldn't set ourselves a hard and fast completion date. These practices are more about the journey than the destination. Obviously, it will become easier as the practices become a habit, but you will still face obstacles from time to time, and this is where constant vigour is required.

Vigilance

The next valuable quality required for the path is vigilance. First, we get inspired by confidence, we then put in wholehearted effort and now we need to become more aware and mindful.

So, what is it that we need to be vigilant about? I would say it is the path itself, our emotional state and our mental, verbal and physical actions. There are many obstacles, both psychological and physical that can lead us away from the path. So, we need to be vigilant of our thoughts, feelings, emotions, body sensations and the places we find ourselves in at all times.

If left unchecked our thoughts can lead us to obsess negatively about the past or the future. When we are focused on the present we can chose to let negative thoughts go and concentrate on the positive and helpful ones. Of course, this takes practice but is possible if we are vigilant. Once your vigilance is lost and your mind is unguarded, it is easy to fall into old unhelpful patterns. This could lead you away from the path and in a direction you really didn't want to travel.

When our five senses come into contact with a sense object, such as smell, taste, sound and so on, a feeling arises within us. Remember I mentioned that there were three types of feelings, namely pleasant, neutral or unpleasant. One of these feelings will arise with each and every experience we have. We need to be vigilant of this fact because pleasant feelings can lead to attachment, unpleasant feelings to aversion and neutral feelings to apathy. Any of these feelings has the potential to distract and disturb the mind.

Emotions can be a huge distraction, especially strong, destructive ones, such as anger, pride, jealousy and so on. This is where we need to be ultra-vigilant because once we are in the grip of a strong emotion we lose all control of rational thinking. Let's take anger as an example, we have all been there, someone says something to make us see red and instantly, without thinking, we open our mouths and a load of abusive words come flying out. This is because we have lost the ability to be responsive, we cannot stop ourselves and simply react. If we are not careful it can quite easily escalate to violence. Of course, once the red mist has cleared, we start feeling regret, but it is a little too late for that.

So, we need to be vigilant of the emotions arising in us and deal with them before they escalate. This can only be done in the present moment. We can't deal with them before they have arisen and, as we know, it is impossible to do once they have taken hold. Being mindful of our emotions in the here and now is the only answer.

We should also be vigilant of our body sensations as well. This gets us out of our heads and into our bodies. These days, we give so much importance to the processes in our brain that we inadvertently block out signals from the body.

Our bodies are extraordinary things, but we tend to take them for granted. When everything is alright with the body, we ignore it, but when there is something wrong with it, we become frustrated.

Being vigilant of our body sensations naturally brings us into the present moment.

It is impossible to feel how the body was yesterday or how it will be tomorrow, you can only feel how it is right at this moment. So, by checking in with our body sensations we are naturally transported into the here and now.

It also allows us to get in touch with our gut feelings. These are intuitions or instincts, as opposed to an opinion based on logical analysis. These gut feelings can tell you that something is wrong in your body, you are in danger, they help you sense when someone needs help or give you a feeling that something is right, even though logically it doesn't make sense. When we fixate so much on our thoughts we miss these gut feelings. Being observant of our bodies helps us reconnect with our gut. So, be vigilant of what your body is telling you – don't ignore your gut feelings.

Finally, we need to be vigilant of our immediate surroundings. Are you aware of what is happening around you at any given time? The way to do this is to engage your senses. Take time to really look, listen, smell and touch. These can only be done in the present moment and so a simple exercise of engaging your senses will bring you into the here and now. Two important aspects of this exercise are walking and talking. When walking, smell the air, listen for any sounds, look around you and feel the ground beneath your feet. Don't just walk, do it mindfully. When talking to others truly listen with an open-mind. Don't try to prejudge what others are going to say. This will help you better understand what the person is trying to communicate, and help you respond in a kind and helpful way.

One of the things that makes these sensory exercises difficult is that the mind wants to judge and criticise the things it is sensing. Once our mind starts thinking or daydreaming, our attention can quickly get distracted, taking us off in a direction we really do not need to go. So, vigilance is required at this time.

Focus

It is so easy to lose our focus; our senses become engaged with something, we get pain in our body, our mind suddenly wanders off or a strong emotion arises, all of these are things that take away our focus.

I have to say that I struggled a lot at school because of a lack of focus. I found looking out of the window daydreaming far more interesting than the lessons. I lost count of how many times the teachers would throw something at my head to gain my attention. It wasn't until I started to meditate that I became more focused.

So, to remain focused we need to develop the ability to concentrate single-pointedly on one thing at a time. Remember what I said earlier? The way to strengthen our minds, to gain focus, is through meditation. The more you meditate, the more you are able to stay focused and your attention becomes stable and undistracted.

Discernment

The final valuable quality I want to explore is discernment. A mind that is confident, has vigour, is vigilant and focused can develop discernment. This helps us determine which thoughts, feelings and emotions are worth following, those we need to let go of and those we need to develop.

With discernment we begin to take responsibility for our actions and our mind. We start to understand what is conducive to a peaceful mind and what is not. We learn to let go of unhelpful thoughts, feelings, emotions, perceptions, habits and motivations. Applying this wisdom leads our mind to a greater sense of peace.

Discernment grows from intuitive and experiential insights. This can be gained through study, analysis and self-inquiry performed in meditation. Studying is an important starting point, but results in just knowledge, which is second hand. Self-inquiry meditation helps turn this knowledge into wisdom. If we don't analyse during our meditation sessions, we will not be able to see what to develop and what to let go.

Confidence, vigour, vigilance, focus and discernment, are key qualities to assist you as you proceed on this path. We need to have conviction that the path is going to bring us peace of mind. Then, once we have this conviction, we need to put in the effort. After that, we need to be mindful about all aspects of the path and ensure we do not lose our focus. Finally, we need to turn what we learn on this path into wisdom and make it part of our very being.

Twelve – Seeing Clearly

This path is not a mystical or religious path; it is a clear way to reduce our physical and emotional suffering and give us peace of mind. But you will not only be helping yourself, you will also be contributing to the wellbeing of those around you and to society as a whole. We live in an interconnected world built upon mutual support. What we do affects others and what they do affects us.

Up to this point I have written about mental training exercises, such as meditation, mindfulness and reflection. I will now introduce lifestyle practices, which enable us to see clearly, live responsibly and stay focused. There are three aspects to this path. They are further broken down into eight practices.

1. Seeing Clearly

View/Understanding

Intention

2. Living Responsibly

> Communication
>
> Action
>
> Livelihood

3. Staying Focused

> Effort
>
> Mindfulness
>
> Meditation

I will take each aspect individually and explore the appropriate ways to approach the eight practices of the path. I use the word appropriate and not right or correct because I feel it is less dogmatic and leaves room for your own input. We cannot always place things into the two extremes of right and wrong, as there is a large grey area between these two. By doing what is appropriate we have given it some thought, weighed up the pros and cons and come to the conclusion that this is the appropriate thing to do at this particular moment. At other times, you may act differently because it requires a different approach. For example, we all know that we should refrain from lying, but there may be an instance when you tell the truth people will be harmed. So, in that situation you may feel it is appropriate not to be fully honest. In other situations, you may choose to tell the truth, but in this situation, it is not appropriate.

These eight practices should not be seen as something we have to do one at a time. We do not start with view and work our way down to concentration. They have to be understood and practiced together.

The first aspect of the path is seeing clearly, which covers view and intention.

View/Understanding

So, what is the view? Appropriate view refers to the understanding that we cause most of our emotional suffering ourselves, the understanding that everything is impermanent and the understanding that things happen due to causes, which in turn lead to consequences. As I have already covered the first two, suffering and impermanence in previous chapters, I will concentrate here on the understanding of cause and effect.

Understanding the view is very important because it allows us to face the right direction. If we start off looking the wrong way it is easy to take the wrong path, and we can quickly get lost, confused and disillusioned.

So, what do we need to understand about cause and effect? It is important to understand that our actions of body, speech and mind have consequences. You may think that, 'I understand that actions of body and speech have consequences, but how can our thoughts?' Before we do any action, it starts off as a thought – first we think and then we act. This thought can be conscious or unconscious, but it is there before any action. So, it is important to realise that our thoughts also have consequences.

Whatever we do and say will become a cause for our future conditions. I am not talking about future lives here; I am talking about this life. We are the architects of our future. This is how we should be thinking. We should not be thinking that our lives are conditioned by some system of reward and punishment meted out by an outside force. This way of thinking is just shirking our responsibilities. Of course, it is easier to blame someone else for our problems, we love doing that, but this will not help us bring about a change for the better in our lives.

Put simplistically, if we act in a kind, caring, helpful and compassionate way, we will be helping to build a good future for ourselves. This is not some metaphysical law, I am just stating the way life is. If we act in a bad way by not caring for others, stealing, lying, cheating, killing and generally acting in a harmful way, people are not going to want to be associated with us or help us when we need it. This is the way of the world. Also, if we are a kind and caring person our conscience will be clear, and this will also reduce our emotional suffering and certainly help us during our meditation and mindful awareness practices.

There is no scientific evidence for this, but just look at your own experiences and I am sure you will see that your actions have consequences. If you kill someone you will be caught and sent to prison or put to death. However, if you are not caught, you will have to carry the torment, anguish and guilt around with you for the rest of your life, fearful every time the doorbell rings. Either way there are consequences for your act of killing.

Having said that, I am not suggesting that if we act in a good way the whole of our life is going to be rosy. Unfortunately, that isn't going to happen, but it will reduce the chances of bad things happening. It will also put us in a better frame of mind to be able to cope with these unfavourable situations when they arise.

We don't live in a bubble, so the actions of others are also going to affect us. Other people's causes and effects overlap our causes and effects until there is a huge web of interconnected causes and effects. So, we have to remember that when something unpleasant befalls us it is the result of a huge number of causes. This will stop us adding anger and frustration to an already difficult situation. It will also prevent us from struggling with something that is beyond our control. This will at the very least reduce some of our emotional suffering.

When we have the appropriate view regarding cause and effect, it encourages us to live an honourable life. This is a life where we take responsibility for our actions because we know it is going to affect our future and the future of all the people we meet.

Before you move on, I would encourage you to look at these questions on cause and effect and reflect on your answers:

Does anything just magically appear?

If you plant a rice seed, what will grow?

Would you expect a banana tree to grow from a rice seed?

Do you have total control over your life or do the actions of others affect you?

When you start to reflect like this you will understand that things can only come into existence due to a cause or causes and not randomly or magically. Every cause will ultimately have an effect. So, all of our actions of body, speech and mind are going to have consequences. This should encourage us to act in a skilful way.

Intention

The next element of the path is intention. What I am talking about here is your motivation and conditioning, as it is these forces that move us into doing actions with our bodies, speech or minds.

This element is divided into three sections: letting go, freedom from ill-will and harmlessness.

Letting go

The first section is sometimes talked about as renunciation, giving something up, rejecting or abandoning, but I think a better way to describe this is the act of letting go. What we are trying to let go of is attachment to, or craving for, sensual objects.

I personally believe renunciation is never going to work. The more we try to renounce something, the more we get ourselves entangled in it. If you are fighting something, you are giving it power. So, in that way, for me, renunciation will not work. This is why I say let it go, because by doing that you are giving it no power and it will begin to disappear on its own. What I mean by letting things go is that we don't get ourselves ensnared by over thinking, judging, comparing or criticising, we don't engage the desire, we allow it to arise, we acknowledge it, let it pass and we move on. Of course, that is easier said than done but this is where our mindful awareness practice helps a lot. If we are present with our thoughts, we will catch the desire as it arises. This gives us the opportunity to follow the desire or let it go.

Clinging to desires is one of the origins of our emotional suffering, but when we try to let things go, a strong feeling inside stops us from succeeding. This happens because we are so attached to our desires. It is never easy to suddenly just let them go, but it certainly is not impossible.

If we believe sensual objects are going to give us true happiness, we will start clinging to them and this will in turn shape our thoughts and actions. We will become attached and our emotional suffering will begin.

It takes time to change our perceptions and it is not going to be easy. We have to slowly start chipping away at our clinging attachment to sensual objects, whether it is to people or belongings. Step by step we reduce their hold on us.

How do we let our clinging desires go? There are several ways, but I believe the best one is to contemplate impermanence. So, try reflecting on these points:

Think about how you looked 10 years ago and how you look now. Is it different?

Think of all the people you have known in your life. How many are still alive?

Look at all the experiences you have had in your life. Have any of them ever lasted, other than in your memory?

By reflecting in this way, you begin to realise the impermanence of things, you understand that everything is temporary and there is nothing solid to get attached to. So, when a clinging desire arises you do not have to hold on to it, you can let it go. Just keep reminding yourself that, 'This is temporary and will pass.'

Freedom from ill-will

This is when we do not have any thoughts of causing others harm.

Ill-will stems from clinging to our ego and can arise when we are unhappy with someone, jealous, have too much pride, anger, have an aversion towards someone and so on. For example when someone, such as our friend, partner or family member has hurt us, and we start wishing bad things to happen to them. Ill-will is often an emotional reaction. It doesn't necessarily follow that we will act upon our ill-will, but as our actions are driven by our thoughts, the potential is always there to do so.

The best way to liberate ourselves from ill-will is to foster the thought that other people, just like us, are fighting against the physical and emotional suffering running through their lives. They also want to be free of this emotional suffering and want only peace of mind. If we think like this, it will cause goodwill to arise within us. So, caring for others' feelings and showing them genuine warmth replaces ill-will with a sense of compassion and kindness.

Now when I talk about caring for others, I am not talking about sympathy or pity, but real empathy. This is when we put ourselves in other people's shoes and truly understand that they wish to be treated kindly and with warmth. They too are struggling to make sense of their lives.

These days, we tend to ration our kindness to people we are friendly with. This way of acting can be selfish and goes part of the way to explain why there is so much ill-will in the world today. You need look no further than the vile comments people post on social media or how some politicians talk about each other to see an all too common manifestation of ill-will.

So, how do we go beyond ill-will and build a feeling of goodwill towards others? One way is to do the following practice, which is a reflection on kindness and is split into three parts, which embraces three types of people we encounter in life: those we are friendly with, those we are not friendly with and the biggest group by far, those we do not care about one way or another. The point of this practice is to open our minds and build friendliness towards all three types of people.

Start by sitting comfortably and lightly closing your eyes. Focus your awareness on the breath flowing in and out of your nose. Don't change the breath in any way, just let it flow naturally.

Now, start reflecting on your friends. This is the easiest way to begin because you already have a certain amount of warmth towards them. Think of a close friend and start to reflect on their positive qualities and their acts of kindness. A note of caution here: try not to use someone you are sexually attracted to because kindness could quite easily turn into lust. It is also recommended that you do not use the same person each time or else you may get attached to them.

By reflecting on your friend's good qualities and kindness, positive feelings will arise. Once this has occurred, you should move away from reflecting on your friend and concentrate on your feelings that have arisen. These feelings should be your primary focus. They should be feelings of warmth and empathy. Spend some time being aware of this warmth and see how happy and peaceful it makes you feel.

Keeping the above feelings in mind, move on to the next type of person, someone you dislike. Picture this person in your mind and examine him or her closely. See the person's pain, *suffering, loneliness and insecurity. See that all he or she really wants is to have a peaceful mind. Now start to radiate the same feelings you had for your friend towards the person you dislike. Project all the respect, warmth and kindness that you can muster.*

Finally, picture a person you pass by everyday but do not care about one way or another. Again, feel this person's pain and see how all he or she is looking for is peace of mind. Radiate your warmth and kindness towards this person and imagine how that makes him or her feel, and in turn, how you feel.

This is a simple way of cultivating respect and warmth for everybody, regardless of whether you know them or not, whether you like them or not. Remember, though, that this is not a reflective exercise that you do only in the privacy of your home. It should be applied to your daily life so that you cultivate a friendly and open attitude towards everyone without discrimination. That of course includes yourself, so if you are feeling a bit low or your self-compassion needs a boost, you can start this practice by radiating warmth and kindness towards yourself.

Harmlessness

You should now have started to have feelings of goodwill towards others. These feelings should move you towards actions that are not harmful. Remember, our mind controls our actions, so feelings of goodwill should lead to more skilful actions.

Everybody wishes to be free of emotional suffering but are often gripped by discontentment, anguish, unease, dissatisfaction and other kinds of suffering. People have their own private suffering, but we should understand that we also play a part in that suffering by not showing compassion for them, by not caring for their well-being and by not seeing that, they, like us are trying to free themselves from all forms of suffering and have peace of mind.

There are various reflections that you can practice that will help you start developing compassion for others.

Do these reflections on the three types of people mentioned in the goodwill section. However, this time choose people who you know are suffering, and radiate compassion towards them.

Again, start your reflection on a friend who you know is going through a rough time. Reflect on that person's suffering directly and then reflect on how, like yourself, your friend wants to be free from pain. You should continue this reflection until a strong feeling of compassion arises within you.

Remember, compassion is not pity or sympathy, but is a form of empathy. Pity and sympathy stem from our own emotions, which are not stable or reliable. Whereas empathy is where you put yourself into another person's shoes and feel what they are feeling. The beauty of this is that you are not projecting your thoughts and prejudices but are actually seeing things from another person's point of view.

Once you start experiencing a strong feeling of compassion for your friend, hold onto it and use it as a standard for the same practice we will now do as we reflect on the two other types of people.

Think of a person you know who is suffering, but whom you dislike, and then reflect on their suffering. See the world through their eyes, try and understand what they are going through. Try to genuinely feel their pain and suffering. Once you have achieved this, start radiating the powerful feeling of compassion you felt before.

When you feel such strong compassion for a person, it is difficult to dislike them anymore because you now understand that they feel suffering, just like you.

Next, think of a person you really have no feelings for one way or another. Start reflecting on how they also have causes for pain, sorrow, anguish and dissatisfaction. Again, once you have truly felt their pain, start radiating compassion towards them. This exercise helps you realise that we are all prone to suffer in the same way, and there really are no strangers in this world.

By doing these reflections, you will slowly be able to open your mind and expand your compassion towards more people in your world. You will start to see that all of us are the same. By doing this reflection you are not necessarily going to be able to directly ease another's suffering, but you are going to be more open to doing so, as your compassion for them grows.

This ends the 'seeing clearly' aspect of the path. Repeatedly check how you are progressing along the path. This can be done during one of your daily reflective sessions.

Thirteen – Living Responsibly

The second aspect of the path is living responsibly. We can achieve this by being mindful of our communication, actions and livelihood.

Communication

Appropriate communication is a big part of this path and can help us live a more responsible life. Traditionally, there are four different aspects of this and they are refraining from lying, divisive speech, using abusive words and gossiping.

I am sure the majority of us wish to live in a kind and compassionate place where people communicate wisely and appropriately, contributing to a more harmonious world. We can go some way in achieving this by being truthful, using words that bring us together, being polite and talking meaningfully. These are skilful ways for us to connect with each other.

Of course, we shouldn't fool ourselves and think that we can always be truthful, polite and meaningful. There are going to be occasions where it makes sense to stretch the truth, talk harshly and spend time in idle chatter.

Let's look at some examples. If a seriously ill person asked you if they are going to die and by telling them the truth you would be making matters worse, it is better to lie to them and allow them to have some peace. Maybe one of your friends has gotten in with the wrong crowd, so you decide to speak divisively and try to break up the group. Your young child is about to put their hand into a fire and out of compassion you speak harshly to stop them. A work colleague is having a rough time and is finding it hard to open up, so you indulge in idle chatter to win their trust, so they can finally feel comfortable to talk about their problems.

All these examples show that appropriate communication isn't always black and white. I think as a rule of thumb, we should ensure that if we do lie, are divisive, talk harshly or gossip it is for the benefit of others and not just for our own selfish gain.

Action

Appropriate action traditionally covers those actions we should refrain from. We are advised to avoid violent acts, to refrain from taking what has not been given, to limit our consumption of intoxicants and to refrain from causing harm through sexual activity. However, I believe the concept of appropriate action should cover all the actions we undertake in our lives. The more we can bring mindfulness to our everyday actions the more our life improves and the impact our life has on others will also grow.

The key point I am making here is to have integrity. I find that the best way for my actions to remain skilful is to keep the view of cause and consequences in the forefront of my mind. Whenever a thought arises I try to gauge whether it will be helpful or harmful and what the consequences are going to be.

This is no easy task and requires us to be mindful of our thoughts.

When we are being mindful it gives us the space to think before we act. An alert mind has the opportunity to override unhelpful or destructive thoughts. It brings awareness into whatever we are intending to do. This is how we can ensure our actions are appropriate and skilful.

Livelihood

This is an important aspect of the path and one we probably do not give a lot of thought to. We should aim to engage in compassionate activity and earn our living in a way that does not cause harm and is ethically positive. Most of us spend a large part of our waking hours at work, so it's important to assess how our work affects us and those around us. We need to work to earn money, without money we cannot survive, this is an unavoidable fact of life. But have you ever stopped to think whether your work is helping or harming? Come to think about it, have you ever stopped to think what is an ethically appropriate livelihood at all?

Do you have an appropriate livelihood? It may not be as black and white as you first think. You may sell guns to the army to keep the country safe, but those guns could fall into the hands of a terrorist and be used to kill innocent people. You may make cars, so people can get around, but one of those cars may be involved in an accident and someone is killed. You may make rope and it is used by someone to commit suicide. I know I have given extreme examples here, but I just want to get you thinking about the consequences of your livelihood.

It would be impossible to examine all the possible effects our work has in the world, but we should certainly contemplate whether we are causing harm in any obvious or direct ways, to humans, to animals, and to the planet.

I recently met a young biologist and he had a dilemma. He had just graduated and was looking for work, but every job he applied for required testing on animals. He said he just couldn't bring himself to kill animals, even if it meant he might discover a new way to help humans. Our choices are not always clear cut, we need to think very carefully about what path we decide to take. We should consider the consequences, to ourselves and to others, of any choice we make.

I fully understand that we need to work to earn money and sometimes we have to do the jobs we find unpalatable. So, I am not being judgemental here. I am just pointing out that we have to be mindful of our livelihoods, and reiterating the fact that actions have consequences.

Pause here for a moment and give your livelihood some thought.

Is it ethical?

Am I forced to do things that go against my redlines?

Do I fully understand the consequences of my livelihood?

Living responsibly highlights the importance of acting in an appropriate way physically, verbally and psychologically. If we don't, we can often inadvertently cause conflict and bitterness amongst the people we come into contact with. We must integrate this part of the path into our daily lives and be constantly mindful of the actions we are carrying out.

Each day, in your daily reflective session, look at what you have done, thought and said during the day. Reflect on these points:

Was my speech positive or negative? Was it kind and helpful or unkind and unhelpful?

Did my actions cause peace or tension? Did I upset anyone with my actions today? Could have I acted in a more helpful way?

This constant review of our behaviour will help us change and, in turn, live more harmoniously and responsibly

Fourteen – Staying Focused

The final aspect of the path is staying focused, which is achieved by effort, mindfulness and concentration.

Effort

Effort has been mentioned several times throughout this book and there is good reason for that. Without applying effort, we are not going to reach any of the goals we set ourselves. Here I wish to highlight the effort required to avoid harmful acts and develop helpful ones.

These are split into four parts, namely the effort to avoid, the effort to overcome, the effort to develop and the effort to maintain.

This is a list of the harmful acts we need to avoid and overcome.

- Killing
- Stealing
- Sexual misconduct
- Lying

- Divisive speech
- Harsh words
- Gossiping
- Greed
- Ill-will
- Inappropriate view

We have to put in a great effort in order to avoid these ten harmful actions. This is achieved by setting ourselves boundaries and ensuring we stay within them. In my own case some of them came easy to me and others were fairly difficult, but by putting in the effort and setting myself redlines, I manage to avoid them for the most part. But none of us are perfect, so we shouldn't be too hard on ourselves.

The next place we apply effort is to overcome the harmful acts that have already arisen. This one is a little trickier, particularly if they have already become a habit. The first thing I suggest you do is to rate the above list of harmful actions from one to ten – one being the act you do the most and ten being the one you do the least. You can also keep track of this during your daily reflection session. Be honest with yourself, even if it is painful, or there will be no point in doing the exercise. Now, start with number one on your list and each day set an intention to refrain from doing the act. This exercise will help keep it in the forefront of your mind. If you do unwittingly perform a harmful deed, don't get frustrated, just reaffirm your intention. This is where mindful awareness comes into its own because you are going to have to be vigilant of your actions. Slowly work through the list until you feel confident that you have by and large overcome them.

The set of skilful acts we have to develop and maintain are the opposite of the harmful acts.

- Compassion
- Generosity
- Self-restraint
- Truthfulness
- Kind speech
- Pleasant words
- Helpful words

- Contentment
- Goodwill
- Appropriate view

The third effort is to develop skilful acts that have not yet arisen. Again, the perfect time to think about and cultivate these helpful deeds is during your daily reflection session. If you review each day which actions have been helpful, and which have been harmful, you will see a pattern emerge. You will then be able to see what you need to work on.

During your reflection session, write down the ten helpful acts on a piece of paper. Then grade them from one to ten - ten being the act that comes naturally to you and one being the act that you have to cultivate. Those you grade from one to five are the ones you should work on. At regular intervals, do the grading again. Note your progress every time and recommit to developing the helpful acts you need to work on.

The final effort is to maintain the helpful actions that have already arisen. This follows on from the previous effort. There, you contemplated which helpful acts you need to work on. Now focus on the ones that come naturally to and need no great work. You should also remain mindful of these helpful deeds, so they can become an even deeper habit. It is no good lying sometimes and telling the truth at other times; stealing sometimes and not stealing other times; getting totally drunk one day and then saying you don't drink another day; or being faithful sometimes and cheating on your partner at other times. These helpful acts must become natural and spontaneous. It needs a great amount of effort to keep these going, because if you do not stay watchful, they can easily drift away from you. Perseverance and vigilance are key here.

During one of your reflection sessions, look at the list you made in the last section and note the helpful actions you graded between six and ten. Check to see if you really have achieved them, and it's not just wishful thinking. If you recognise them in your daily life, then stay mindful of them, and direct your effort towards maintaining them.

Mindfulness

Whether we are on the path or not, we still should try to be mindful, and maintain an awareness of where our actions are taking us. If we don't we are not going to find the peace of mind we are searching for. So, let's look at the different aspects of the path I have laid out and examine how we can approach it mindfully.

We cannot just jump into our practices without first having an appropriate view. Of course, cultivating positive experience is what our practices are all about, but if we have no clear picture of where we are going and why we can quite easily flounder. We need to know what and why we are doing any practice and see clearly how it will fit into our lives. We need to study and think to gain a clear picture in our mind before we dive into our practice. A firm and stable foundation is required. Mindfully setting our intentions for travelling on this path and implementing a meditation practice is a wonderful way to become motivated. It allows us to stay on track. It is therefore important to have well thought-out intentions and stay mindful of them.

Mindless speech can often divide people and make them feel disconnected. In contrast mindful speech helps us heal rifts and make better connections with each other. I feel that if we practice mindful listening, which is being totally engaged with the other person and allowing them to finish their sentences, mindful speech arises naturally, and we can enjoy genuine dialogue.

We need to mindfully check in with ourselves during the day to ensure our actions, physically, verbally and mentally, are not harmful to ourselves or others. This strengthens our practice, so we maintain the goal of responsible living.

Usually livelihood equates with survival – earning money so we can live. But when we are being mindful of our work we can see that it is also about contributing to the common good. It is not just about money, it is also about giving back to society. We have to be mindful of any harm we may be causing ourselves and others.

Of course, we need to put effort into whatever we are doing on the path to ensure success, but there is such thing as too much effort. We need to be mindful of the amount of effort we are putting in. If the effort is causing tension, it is too much. If the effort is not producing any results, it is not enough. Be mindful of how much effort you are putting into the path and your practices.

When we are being mindful we are fully aware of, but not tangled up in, the various aspects of our experience – the emotional, the physical, the spiritual as well as the social. Mindfulness covers our complete engagement with life.

Meditation

If we wish for a mind that is at peace we need to learn how to focus single-mindedly on an object of meditation. However, what I want to highlight here is a particular type of one-pointedness. It is a wholesome type of concentration. A killer about to murder his victim, a soldier on the battlefield or a burglar about to break into your home all act with a concentrated mind, but they cannot be classed as a wholesome one-pointedness.

When our mind is not focused it flaps around like a fish on dry land. It simply cannot stay still and jumps from one idea to another, from one thought to another, there is absolutely no control. Such a distracted mind is consumed by worries and concerns about what has happened or may happen in the future. It doesn't see the whole picture and distorts reality.

But a mind that has been trained in meditation can remain focused on its object without any distractions. This allows the mind to become calm, clear and open. This calm, openness can then be taken off the cushion and used in the outside world. This will allow us to stay single-mindedly aware of all stages of this path.

There are many different meditations throughout this book that will help focus your mind on a single object if you practice them regularly. Here, I want to introduce you to a meditation practice that will help you let go of disturbing thoughts, stop you over-thinking and assist you in taking a break from your busy mind. This will allow the mind to become calm, open and single-pointedly focused.

Come to Go Meditation

Sit on a chair, or lay down somewhere quiet and gently close your eyes.

Breathe in slowly and deeply through your nose - hold the breath.

Now gently release the air out through your mouth.

Again, slowly breathe in – hold - now gently release the air.

One more time, slowly breathe in - hold and then gently release the air.

Now breath naturally and bring your focus to your breath entering and leaving your body.

Feel your chest rising on the in-breath and falling on the out-breath.

(pause for 30 seconds)

I want you to visualise yourself sitting on the bank of a stream. Take a moment and listen to the stream gently flowing over the rocks - listen to the birds singing in the trees - smell the beautiful flowers growing along the bank - feel the warmth of the sun on your face

(pause for 10 seconds)

Feel yourself starting to become calm and relaxed

(pause for 10 seconds)

For the next few minutes, take each thought that enters your mind and place it on a leaf and let it slowly float down the stream. Do this with every thought – whether there pleasurable, painful or neutral. Even if you have happy thoughts, place them on a leaf and let them float down the stream.

(pause for 30 seconds)

Just let your thoughts come and go.

(pause for 30 seconds)

If your thoughts momentarily stop, just continue to watch the stream gently flowing. Sooner or later, your thoughts will start up again.

(Pause for 30 seconds).

Allow the stream to flow at its own pace. Don't try to speed it up or rush your thoughts along. You're not trying to hurry the leaves along or 'get rid' of your thoughts. You are allowing them to come and go at their own pace.

(pause for 30 seconds)

If your mind says, "This feels silly," "I'm bored," or "I'm not doing this right" place those thoughts on leaves and let them float off.

(pause for 30 seconds)

If a thought comes up again, gently put it on another leaf and watch it float off again.

(pause for 30 seconds)

If a difficult or painful feeling arises, simply acknowledge it. Say to yourself, "I notice myself having a feeling of boredom/impatience/frustration." Place those thoughts on leaves and allow them to float off.

(pause for 30 seconds)

From time to time, your thoughts may distract you from being fully present in this meditation. Don't worry, this is normal. As soon as you realise that you have become side-tracked, gently bring your attention back to sitting by the stream.

(pause for 30 seconds)

There may be other things in your life you wish to let go of, such as memories, painful experiences, attachment to people, whatever it is, just place it on a leaf and let it go gently floating down the stream.

(pause for 30 seconds)

We are now coming to the end of this practice, but before we finish, I would like you to focus your awareness on what it was like for you to engage in this visualisation meditation? If you found yourself struggling to remain fully present and mindful, don't worry, be patient and compassionate with yourself. This practice becomes easier the more you do it.

(pause for 30 seconds)

When you are ready, and there is no rush, I want you to very slowly open your eyes and gently introduce yourself back into the world.

****

Following this path is not easy because many of the things we have to change or let go of are very dear to us. We are passionate about them and have often invested an awful lot of time cultivating them. Letting these unhelpful things go can disturb us. Therefore, change takes diligence, discipline and mindful awareness. We have to understand each of the eight steps and then implement them. They have to become a part of our lives; only then will our minds be at ease and we will gradually reduce our emotional suffering and start to experience the true peace of mind we have been desperately searching for.

Fifteen – Encouragement

Although this is the end of the book, it is only the beginning of your journey of inner discovery. We cannot meditate, be mindful, reflect on our lives or do any of the practices mentioned in this book for a few months and then declare that we have finished. Each day our thoughts, feelings and emotions change and so will our practice. I have personally been practicing for over 40 years and still I regularly discover different aspects of my mind. It is a lifetime's work.

So, please do not read this book and then sit back and say job done. If you do, you will never truly find peace of mind, and remember, that was the goal I mentioned at the start of the book.

We all have the potential to live peaceful, productive lives, we just need to make the effort to sort out our inner world. Once we do that, we will naturally start to see changes in the way we experience and engage with the outer world.

If you have read this book quickly, you have read it wrong. It isn't a book to read once and then put to one side. It needs to be read several times and then used as a reference book. The practices I have mentioned should become your life long companions and guides for cultivating and reviving the experience of inner peace. They should be looked upon as best friends who are always there in your hour of need.

If you have any doubts, questions, comments or need encouragement please feel free to email me at <u>buddhismguide@yahoo.com</u>

Good luck with your journey towards an open awareness and an open mind!